W9-ARK-863

Capron's Pocket Internet

4001 SITES

H. L. Capron

Prentice Hall
Upper Saddle River, New Jersey 07458

For C. L. B.

Copyright © 2000 by Prentice Hall, Inc.
Upper Saddle River, New Jersey 07458

All rights reserved. No part of this book may be used or repro-
duced in any form or by any means without written permission
from the Publisher.

Prentice-Hall International (UK) Limited, London
Prentice-Hall of Australia Pty. Limited, Sydney
Prentice-Hall Canada, Inc., Toronto
Prentice-Hall Hispanoamericana, S.A., Mexico
Prentice-Hall of India Private Limited, New Delhi
Prentice-Hall of Japan, Inc., Tokyo
Pearson Education Asia Pte. Ltd., Singapore
Editora Prentice-Hall do Brasil, Ltda., Rio de Janeiro

ISBN   0-201-61195-3

Printed in the United States of America.

10 9 8 7 6 5 4 3 2

Pocket Start

How much do I need to know in order to use the Internet?

Not much. That is a good part of the reason for its popularity. The best way to get started is to have someone give you a demonstration. When you see how easy it is, you will want to begin clicking and linking yourself.

Clicking and linking?

Yes. Use a mouse to click on a bit of colored text or a small image—the link—and you will see on your screen the web site—from another computer—that the link represents. The World Wide Web, an Internet subset usually called just "the Web," is a collection of web sites, information from other computers that you can see on your own computer screen. Once you get started, you can indeed just click and link from site to site. The total set of links is seen as a giant spider's web, hence the name Web.

You said "once you get started." How does that happen?

If you are in a computer environment—a school, a library, a workplace—the hardware and software to access the Internet are probably already in place. If you want to access the Internet from your own personal computer, the only other hardware you need is a *modem* so that you can make a physical communications link via your telephone system. (There is also the possibility of linking up via cable or some other method, but the telephone is still the most common way.) The software you need for your own computer is called a *browser*, because you will be using it to "browse" the Internet. But you need access to another computer, a bigger computer called a *server*. You could think of the server as a sort of gateway; it has the software that makes the connection to the Internet. Once all these items are in place, you use the browser to contact the server via the modem and the phone system. You will see a *web site* on your screen, usually the browser's own site. It will have the *links* we mentioned, the colored text or images—and now you can begin clicking and linking.

That's it?

That really is it, except that we left out most of the buzzwords. And we should also mention that there is not just one server, but many. You have to pick one and sign up, probably for a monthly fee. But rather than go directly to a server, you might do what many people do—sign up for an *online service* such as America Online, and let them worry about the server.

And the buzzwords?

Just so you have seen the correct terminology, we will describe the whole setup in formal terms.

Internet means, literally, a network of networks. You will use a browser to click on *hypertext*, the kind of text that operates as a link because it represents a *Uniform Resource Locator (URL)*, the address of the *web site*. You can see the URL of the current site in the long skinny window—the address slot—near the top of the browser screen; the URL changes when you link to a new site. A server is more formally called an *Internet Service Provider (ISP)*, and each server uses the software called *Transmission Control Protocol/Internet Protocol (TCP/IP)* to access the Internet and route files. Web site pages are written in a language called *HyperText Markup Language (HTML)*. The first page of a web site is referred to as its *home page*. You can use a *scroll bar* to move up and down the pages of the site. You can click browser *buttons* to move Back to the previous site or Forward again, or, typically, to Print or Reload the page.

I think I need to see a demonstration.
Good idea.

Add just a bit of history, and you will know as much about the Internet as most casual users. The Internet began in 1969 as ARPANet, sponsored by the United States Department of Defense to connect widely scattered computers so that no one enemy bomb could wipe out our computing capabilities. As cold war fears receded and computer networks spread, the network became more public, more generic, and more commercial—and took the new name Internet.

The World Wide Web was conceived by a fellow named Tim Berners-Lee, who was at the time working in a particle physics lab called CERN in Geneva, Switzerland. He thought it would be convenient if he could easily link to the computers of his fellow physicists around the world, so he proceeded to set up the first web. The other major development was the browser, credited to Marc Andreessen, which made possible the easy clicking and linking. That's the bare-bones history.

One more thing. How do I access a web site I've heard about?

If you know the URL (for example, http://www.nike.com), you can type it in your browser's address slot and press Enter. You will be transported to the Nike site. Of course, you are not really going anywhere; it only seems that way. In truth, your browser sends a message to contact the Nike site and its files are sent (via several servers and finally to your server) to your computer.

If you know only the subject matter (say, the name Nike) but not the URL, you can submit the name to software called a *search engine*, which finds sites that match the given name. Search engines are not limited to a name; you could give it several terms, say, "kitchen bathroom designs," and it would return a list of sites matching the terms. The listed sites are presented as links, so you need only click a link name. Several search engines are listed in this book, among site listings, under the heading Internet Search Engines.

Most people soon establish favorite sites and return there again and again to see what's new and to follow new links from there. Your browser will let you save these sites in a *hot list* by clicking a button called Favorites or Bookmarks or some such; in the future you can simply click on the saved link to reach the site.

Is there a table of contents or an index for the Internet?

Not exactly. No one owns the Internet, nor is anyone actually in charge. Several organizations attempt to organize the Internet, producing directories or catalogs. Several are listed in this book, under the heading Internet Directories and Portals. Although none of them would claim to be exhaustive, they offer the Internet in their own way. Any one of them would be a good place to start.

Pocket FAQs

What is a FAQ?

FAQ is an abbreviation for frequently asked question. Most beginners have similar questions. You can get answers before you have even thought of the question.

How many people are connected to the Internet?

There are more than 70 million users worldwide. Over 100,000 new users sign up each month.

Are most users business people? Men? Teenagers?

Studies show that about half of Internet use is for commercial purposes. More men than women are on the Internet, but the gap is closing quickly. Users tend to be youngish but generally not teenagers—late twenties, early thirties. A more distinct trend is that Internet users tend to be rather well educated (more than half have a college degree) and rather well off—middle class or above.

It's called the World Wide Web, but isn't it mostly in the USA?

Yes and no. There is a higher percentage of Web users in the United States than in other countries, but there are still many, many users around the world, in more than 130 different countries, easily enough to make the term *World* Wide Web meaningful.

Why is the Internet so popular?

The Internet offers an extraordinary amount of information on just about any topic. But so does a library. The difference is accessibility. The simple click-on-a-link user interface is attractive to both novices and sophisticated users. What is more, you can click and link right in your own home, at any time or the day or night, and, if you wish, wearing your bathrobe. In addition to being a resource of information, the Internet notches up the convenience level for many services—you need make only a few clicks to check your mutual fund or order tickets or send flowers. Add to this the attractiveness of the graphics, the cleverness of the offerings, and the—usually—reasonable cost of participation, and the package is hard to resist.

What are people doing on the Internet?

Many people are gathering information: for reports, for term papers, for businesses, for hobbies, and much more. Business people use the Internet to provide product information and support to customers, to work remotely with colleagues, to follow what their competitors are doing, to offer marketing and advertising, to send electronic mail, and to send images, sounds, and video. Some people do a fair amount of shopping, especially for books and music, and occasionally for last-minute gifts that can be sent directly to the recipient. Some are playing games or participating in chat rooms and other types of cyberspace communities. But most are *surfing*—just clicking from site to site to see what they happen to come across.

Pocket Tips

My browser looks pretty ordinary, mostly gray.
The default browser look is plain vanilla, but you can use the Preferences menu on your browser to change the colors of the links, the followed links (ones already visited), and the background. You can also change the font and even the language.

Anything else?
You can set e-mail and security options to suit your convenience, and even change the home page that comes up when you use the browser to access the Internet. Under the browser's Help menu, you can find extensive information about how the browser works and how to configure it. But keep in mind that these are options; the browser works just fine if you do none of these things.

I usually enjoy the visual aspects of a site, but sometimes I am just looking for specific information and get tired of waiting for all the fancy graphics to load.
Check your browser's options list. You can control whether or not images are automatically downloaded with the site; that is, you can specify "Text only." This will speed up site loading significantly.

You can, of course, go back to including graphics whenever you wish. Also, most sites include a Text-only option on the opening page.

I am worried about catching a virus from the Internet.

First, your computer cannot catch a virus if you are just looking. Surfing from one web site to another is perfectly safe. You can even safely fill out forms or supply information in other ways if you wish. However, your computer can catch a virus if you download a program from a web site, or any place else on the Internet, and execute it. Although it is generally safe to download software from major vendors, you are taking a risk if you use software from an unknown—and thus unreliable—source.

Just how safe is it to give out my credit card number in order to make a purchase from a web site?

At this point, probably no one would guarantee across-the-board safety. However, several well-known vendor sites encrypt (scramble so that it is unreadable by others) the data you send from your computer to theirs, and they are willing to guarantee its security. If you feel uneasy about this, then get product information from the site and use your telephone to place the order by phone.

I see counters on several sites but not on the more sophisticated commercial sites. Don't they care how many people visit their sites?

They care, all right. But they want much more information than can be provided by a simple counter, which merely records the number of visits, not even the number of visitors. A number of software packages are available to monitor a web site, providing statistics such as usage by server and country, the parts of the site visited, and the peak hours of access to the site. All of this, of course, is done without the site visitor being aware of it. Most important, the software can also determine from what site you have just come. This information can, among other things, reveal the sites where clickable advertising banners are most effective.

I see some great-looking images on web sites that I'd like to have, and maybe even use on my own home page. How can I get them?

There are several ways to capture images that you see on the screen. But first, note that you cannot help yourself to just any image on the screen; to do so could be a copyright infringement. But some images have been made freely available.

The easiest way to capture an image, if you have a browser such as Netscape or Internet

Explorer, is to rest the mouse over the desired image and click the right mouse button. This will cause a menu to appear. Now click the left mouse button on the Save option and choose a directory and name for the file. If you want to capture an entire screen, one which probably has several images, you can use screen capture software.

I know a little about HTML and would like to study how some of the sites I view were written.

Most browsers have an option called View Source. Simply click it and the HTML source code for the current site will show on the screen.

How can I find out someone's e-mail address?

First we must eliminate the possibility of finding the private e-mail address of a celebrity. Their addresses are no more available than their telephone numbers. If you want the e-mail address of someone you know, the most straightforward—and probably fastest—way is to ask the person. Some online services will let you, as a member, look up other members by name, but success depends on whether the other person is a member and, if so, if he or she has filed something akin to a member profile. You can try submitting the person's name to a search engine; a site that carries the person's name may also point to an e-mail address or to someone else who might have it. Some sites, notably WhoWhere and Switchboard, perform e-mail address searches. It should be noted that if the person guards his or her e-mail address, it is unlikely that any of these approaches will work.

How can I get rid of junk mail?

This is one of the toughest issues on the Internet and there are no definitive answers. The easiest way to avoid junk e-mail is the same way you avoid ordinary junk mail or junk telephone calls: hide. If you do not reveal your home address or phone number casually, then you understand that you don't give out your e-mail address casually either. Prevention is the best cure. Bear in mind that each place you leave your e-mail address— chat rooms, web vendors, newsgroups, contests, registration, and so on—is one more place that your e-mail address can be harvested and sold by others.

Once the junk mail starts coming in, you can attempt to stem the tide in various ways. If you belong to an online service such as America Online, find out what measures the service takes to reduce junk mail for its members. You can probably report the offending sender's e-mail address and, given sufficient complaint volume, the service may cut off that sender's access. But don't count on it. A high-volume sender has probably already moved on. Finally, you can buy your own filter software to control which e-mail addresses you will accept messages from.

Pocket Dictionary

Applet A small program that can provide animation such as dancing icons and scrolling banners on a web site.

ARPANet The network, established in 1969 by the Department of Defense, that eventually became the Internet.

Authoring software Software that lets a user make a web page without any having knowledge of HTML; the software converts specifications to HTML.

Backbone The major communications links that tie Internet servers across wide geographical areas.

Background On a web site, the screen appearance behind the text and images. A background is often a plain color, or a color with some texture to it, or perhaps an image or set of images.

Bandwidth The number of frequencies that can fit on one communications line or link at the same time, or the capacity of the communications link.

Banner ad A web site advertisement, often in the shape of a rectangle, that, when clicked, sends the user to the advertised site, called an *affiliate*. A *live banner* lets a user get more information about a product without leaving the current site.

Boolean logic Regarding search engines, a mathematical system that can be used to narrow the search by using operators such as AND, OR, and NOT.

Browser Software used to access the Internet.

CERN The name of the site of the particle physics lab where Dr. Tim Berners-Lee worked when he invented the World Wide Web; sometimes called the birthplace of the Web.

Cookie An entry in a file stored on the user's hard drive that reflects activity on the Internet. For example, a site that sells a product or service may record a cookie indicating what parts of the site a user visited and, based on this, may guide the user or offer certain services on subsequent visits.

Clickable image Any image that has instructions embedded in it so that clicking on it initiates some kind of action or result, usually transferring to another site or another location within the same site. Also called a *hyperregion*.

Click through A reference to users who leave the current Internet site for a site advertised on the current site.

Context sensitive A reference to Web advertisements that are related to the subject matter on the screen.

Cyberspace A term coined by science fiction author William Gibson to describe the whole range of information resources available through computer networks.

Data compression Making a large data file smaller by temporarily removing nonessential but space-hogging items such as tab marks and double-spacing. Compressed files take up less space on a server or hard drive and travel faster over a network.

Domain name The unique name that identifies an Internet Service Provider site. The Internet is made up of hundreds of thousands of computers and networks; each site has its own domain name or unique address. Domain names always have two or more parts separated by dots, for example, netscape.com.

Download In a networking environment, to receive data files from another computer, probably a larger computer or a server. Contrast with *Upload*.

Digital subscriber line (DSL) A service that uses advances electronics to send data over conventional copper telephone wires.

E-mail (electronic mail) Sending written messages from one computer to another.

Electronic commerce Buying and selling over the Internet; more commonly called *e-commerce*.

Extranet A network of two or more intranets.

FAQ An acronym for frequently asked questions. FAQs are online documents that list and answer the most common questions on a particular subject.

Firewall A dedicated computer whose sole purpose is to talk to the outside world and decide who gains entry to a company's private network or intranet.

Flaming Sending insulting e-mail messages, often by large numbers of people in response to spamming. A flame war occurs when two or more users flame each other in an escalating manner that threatens to continue unabated.

Frames The capability of some browsers to display pages of a site in separate sections, each of which may operate independently.

FTP A set of rules for transferring files from one computer to another. Most browsers support using FTP by typing the URL in the browser's address slot.

GIF An acronym for Graphics Interchange Format, a graphics file format that compresses files so that they can be transmitted quickly over a network.

Gopher An Internet subsystem that lets a user find files through a series of narrowing menus.

Graphical user interface (GUI) An image-based computer interface in which the user sends directions to the operating system by selecting icons from a menu or manipulating icons on the screen by using a pointing device such as a mouse.

Home page The first page of a web site.

Hot list A list of names and URLs of favorite web sites. Most browsers support hot lists, called bookmarks or favorites or something similar. Once a site is placed on the hot list, a user can access it quickly by clicking on its name.

HTML See *HyperText Markup Language*.

HTTP See *HyperText Transfer Protocol*.

Hyperregion An icon or image that can be clicked to cause a link to another web site. Also called a *clickable image*.

Hypertext Text that can be clicked to cause a link to another web site; hypertext is usually distinguished by a different color and perhaps underlining.

HypterText Markup Language(HTML) A programming language used to write documents containing hypertext, in particular, pages for the Web.

HyperText Transfer Protocol (HTTP) A set of rules that provide the means of communicating on the World Wide Web by using links. Note "http" as the beginning of each web address.

Icon A small picture on a computer screen; it represents a computer activity or file.

Image map A graphic divided so that when a particular region is clicked, it calls up a web page associated with that particular region. On a site offering national information such as weather, for example, clicking on a particular state on an image map of the United States calls up the appropriate page for that state.

Inline image In HTML, an image that is referenced right in the HTML code and whose file is loaded with the HTML code. The image is displayed on the same page as text.

Internet A public communications network once used primarily by businesses, governments, and academic institutions but now also used by individuals via various private access methods.

Internet Service Provider (ISP) An entity that offers, for a fee, a server computer and the software needed to access the Internet.

Internet Tax Freedom Act A federal law that imposes a three-year moratorium (beginning in October 1998) on taxes imposed on the Internet, and calls for a committee to study the matter.

Intranet A private Internet-like network internal to a certain company.

ISDN Integrated Services Digital Network, which transmits data at 128,000 bps. ISDN requires special equipment, is somewhat complicated to set up and somewhat expensive, but it is very speedy and widely available.

ISP See *Internet Service Provider*.

Java A network-friendly programming language, derived from the C++ language, that allows software to run on many different platforms. In particular, Java is used to write small animations called *applets*.

JPEG Acronym for Joint Photographic Experts Group, an industry committee that developed a compression standard for still images. JPEG refers to the graphics file format that uses this compression standard. JPEG files on the Web have the file extension .JPG.

Lurking Reading messages in newsgroups without writing any.

MIME An acronym for Multipurpose Internet Mail Extension, an Internet protocol that allows users to send binary files across the Internet as attachments to e-mail messages. This includes graphics, photos, sound and video files, and formatted text documents.

Mirror A site that is identical to another site, that is, it offers an alternative way to access the same files. A mirror site is used when a site is so popular that the volume of users accessing it keeps others from getting through.

MPEG An acronym for Motion Picture Experts Group, a set of widely accepted digital video and audio standards.

Multimedia Software that typically presents information with text, illustrations, photos, narration, music, animation, and film clips.

Netiquette An informal code of appropriate behavior in network communications.

Newsgroup An informal network of computers that allows the posting and reading of messages in groups that focus on specific topics. More formally called *Usenet*.

Packet A portion of a message to be sent to another computer via data communications. Each packet is individually addressed. The packets may take different routes and are reassembled into the original message once they reach their destination.

Plug-in Software that can be added to a browser to enhance its functionality.

PNG Acronym for Portable Network Graphics, a graphics file format that is in the public domain and is gradually replacing the GIF standard.

Portal A web site that is used as a gateway or guide to the Internet.

Push technology Software that automatically sends—pushes—information from the Internet to a user's personal computer. Also called *webcasting*.

Search engine Software that lets a user specify search terms that can be used to find web sites that include those terms. The search engine provides a list of the results in hypertext, which means a user can click on any item in the list to go to that site.

Server A computer used to access the Internet; it has special software that uses the Internet protocol.

Shockwave A set of programs that can be added to a browser as a plug-in, allowing the browser to present animated files. Typical applications of Shockwave are games, animated logos, and advertising.

Spamming Mass advertising on the Internet, usually by using software especially designed to send solicitations to users via e-mail.

Streaming Downloading live audio, video, and animation content.

Tag In HTML, a command that performs a specific function.

TCP/IP See *Transmission Control Protocol/Internet Protocol*.

Tile In reference to a screen background, particularly on a web site, spreading a pattern down and across the screen to make a complete background.

Transmission Control Protocol/Internet Protocol (TCP/IP) A standardized protocol permitting different computers to communicate via the Internet.

Uniform Resource Locator (URL) The unique address of a web page or other file on the Internet.

Upload In a networking environment, to send a file from one computer to another, usually to a larger computer or a host computer. Contrast with *Download*.

URL See *Uniform Resource Locator*.

Usenet An informal network of computers that allows the posting and reading of messages in groups that focus on specific topics. Also called *newsgroups*.

Virtual Private Network (VPN) Technology that uses the public Internet backbone as a channel for private data communication. VPNs use *tunneling*, also called *encapsulation*, as a way to transfer data between two similar networks over an intermediate network by enclosing one type of data packet protocol into the packet of another protocol.

Web See *World Wide Web*.

Web site An individual location on the World Wide Web.

Webcasting Software that automatically sends—pushes—information from the Internet to a user's personal computer. Also called *push technology*.

Webmaster The administrator responsible for the management and often the design of a World Wide Web site.

World Wide Web (WWW or the Web) An Internet subset of sites with text, images, and sounds; most web sites provide links to related topics.

Contents

Note: We have not included http:// in site addresses. Most browsers will automatically supply it when you type in the rest of the address. In the few cases in which they do not, simply add http:// to the front of the site address.

4001 Sites

Accounting

If it is true that an accounting major's main concern is the CPA exam, then there is help here. There are also a number of sites for the accounting professional. See also Taxes.

■ **Accountant Courses on the Web**
www.utexas.edu/world/lecture/acc/

■ **Accountant's Resource**
bx.com/mall/account.htm

■ **Accounting Firms Associated**
www.afai.com/

■ **Accounting Net**
accountingnet.com/

■ **Accounting Principals**
www.accountingprincipals.com/

■ **Accounting Professionals'
Resource Center**
www.kentis.com/

■ **Accounting Professors' Page**
www.rutgers.edu/Accounting/raw/internet/
teach.htm

■ **Accounting Resources**
icewall.vianet.on.ca/pages/hutton/account.
html

■ **Accounting.org**
www.accounting.org/

■ **CPAnet**
www.cpanet.com/

■ **CyberAccountant**
www.cyber-cpa.com/

■ **Electronic Accountant**
www.electronicaccountant.com/

■ **How to Apply for the CPA Exam**
www.wiseguides.com/cpabds.htm

■ **List of CPA Firms**
www.cpafirms.com/index.html

■ **Online Accountant**
cpawebsite.com/

■ **Research Institute of America**
www.riatax.com/

■ **Tax News Network**
www.taxnews.com/tnn_public/

Agriculture

Much serious stuff, mostly from the government or organizations, in this list.

■ **AgriBiz**
www.agribiz.com/

■ **Agribusiness Assistant**
www.trace-sc.com/agri/menu.htm

■ **Agriculture Economics Journals**
www.sciencekomm.at/journals/economic.
html

■ **Agriculture Online**
www.agriculture.com/

■ **Agriculture Virtual Library**
www.vlib.org/Agriculture.html

■ **AgriSurf**
www.agrisurf.com/

■ **Alliance for Sustainability**
www.mtn.org/iasa/

■ **American Crop Protection
Association**
www.acpa.org/

■ **ArboricultureOnline**
spectre.ag.uiuc.edu/~isa/

■ **Cybersteed**
www.cybersteed.com/

■ **Dairy Network**
www.dairynetwork.com/

■ **Department of Agriculture**
www.usda.gov/

■ **Farm and Ranch Business Center**
www.traderivers.com/farmranch/index.html

■ **Flora of China**
flora.harvard.edu/china/

■ **Fruit Facts**
www.crfg.org/pubs/frtfacts.html

■ **GrainNet**
www.grainnet.com/BreakingNews/index.
html

■ **HayNet**
www.dairynetwork.com/

■ **Homefarm**
www.traderivers.com/farmranch/index.html

■ **House Committee on Agriculture**
www.house.gov/agriculture/

■ **Lamb Watch**
lambwatch.we.mediaone.net/

■ **Moo Milk**
www.moomilk.com/

■ **National Agricultural Library**
www.nalusda.gov/

■ **National Agricultural Statistics
Service**
www.usda.gov/nass/

■ **Not Just Cows**
www.snymor.edu/~drewwe/njc/splash.htmlx

■ **Seeds of Life**
www.versicolores.ca/SeedsOfLife/

■ **Small Farm Resource**
www.farminfo.org/

■ **The Coop**
www.the-coop.org/index.html

■ **The Eggman**
www.hughson.com/eggman/

■ **Urban Agriculture Notes**
www.cityfarmer.org/
■ **Virtual Orchard**
orchard.uvm.edu/

Animals and Birds

The sites in this list provide every kind of information to help you care for your domestic pet. And there are a few sites for nondomestic animals and birds.

■ **American Kennel Club**
www.akc.org/
■ **American Rare Breed Association**
www.arba.org/
■ **Attracting and Feeding Hummingbirds**
aggie-horticulture.tamu.edu/extension/
pruning/pruning.html
■ **Bird Web**
www.abdn.ac.uk/~nhi019/intro.html
■ **Care for Pets**
www.avma.org/care4pets/default.htm
■ **Cat Fanciers**
www.fanciers.com/
■ **CyberPet**
www.cyberpet.com/

■ **Cybersteed**
www.cybersteed.com/

■ **Doggie Information**
www.bulldog.org/dogs/

■ **FatCat**
www.fatcats.com/

■ **House Rabbit**
www.rabbit.org/

■ **Hummingbirds**
www.derived.net/hummers/

■ **Kitten Rescue**
www.kittenrescue.org/

■ **National Audubon Society**
www.audubon.org/

■ **Nestbox**
www.nestbox.com/

■ **NetVet**
netvet.wustl.edu/

■ **Oriental Birds**
www.orientalbirdclub.org/

■ **Pet Channel**
www.thepetchannel.com/

■ **PetsForum Group**
www2.cichlidae.com/

■ **Petz Central**
www.dogz.com/

■ **South Florida Birding**
www.southfloridabirding.com/index.htm

Architecture

■ **Tame Beast**
www.tamebeast.com/

■ **TravelDog**
www.traveldog.com/

■ **Virtual Pet Cemetery**
www.lavamind.com/pet.html

Architecture

There are fewer architecture sites than you might expect, but the ones that do exist have rich content and are well worth a visit.

■ **Ace Architects**
www.aceland.com/

■ **AEC Info**
www.aecinfo.com/

■ **American Institute of Architecture Students**
www.aiasnatl.org/

■ **American Institute of Architects**
www.aecinfo.com/

■ **Ancient City of Athens**
www.indiana.edu/~kglowack/athens/

■ **ArchE+/BBZine**
www.usaor.net/users/archeplus/BBZine.html

■ **ArchINFORM**
www.archinform.de/

■ **Architects, Engineers, Contractors**
www.aecinfo.com/

■ **Architecture and Building Links**
www.architecturelinks.com/

■ **Architecture Resources on the Internet**
fbox.vt.edu:10021/H/hmock/arch/arch.html

■ **Barn Journal**
museum.cl.msu.edu/barn/

■ **Buckminster Fuller**
www.pbs.org/wnet/bucky.cgi

■ **Cyburbia**
www.arch.buffalo.edu/pairc/

■ **Frank Lloyd Wright Foundation**
www.franklloydwright.org/

■ **Frank Lloyd Wright**
www.mcs.com/~tgiesler/flw_home.htm#links

■ **Hillier Group**
www.hillier.com/

■ **Irish Architecture Online**
www.archeire.com/

■ **Jones and Jones**
www.jonesandjones.com

■ **Lundstrom**
www.lundstromarch.com/

■ **Medieval Art and Architecture**
www1.pitt.edu/~medart/index.html

■ **Plan Net**
www.plannet.com/

■ **Totem**
www.totemweb.com/

Artificial Intelligence

Artificial intelligence could be considered the high end of computer science. Many of these sites contain sophisticated content.

■ **Applied Artificial Intelligence**
www.tandf.co.uk/jnls/aai.htm

■ **Artificial Intelligence FAQs**
www.cs.cmu.edu/Groups/AI/html/faqs/ai/
ai_general/top.html

■ **Artificial Intelligence Group–JPL**
www-aig.jpl.nasa.gov/

■ **Artificial Intelligence Information Bank**
aiintelligence.com/

■ **Artificial Intelligence Introduction**
tqd.advanced.org/2705/

■ **Artificial Intelligence Library**
www.cs.reading.ac.uk/people/dwc/ai.html

■ **Artificial Intelligence Repository**
www.cs.cmu.edu/Groups/AI/html/air.html

■ **Artificial Intelligence Resources**
ai.iit.nrc.ca/ai_point.html

- **Artificial Intelligence Tools**
www.wspc.com/journals/ijait/ijait.html

- **Context in Artificial Intelligence**
tqd.advanced.org/2705/

- **Evaluation of Intelligent Systems**
eksl-www.cs.umass.edu/eis/

- **Game AI**
www.gameai.com/ai.html

- **Journal of Artificial Intelligence Research**
www.cs.washington.edu/research/jair/home.html

- **Journal of Artificial Intelligence Systems**
www.brunel.ac.uk/~hssrjis/

- **MIT Artificial Intelligence Lab**
libraries.mit.edu/docs/

- **Outsider's Guide to Artificial Intelligence**
www.mcs.net/~jorn/html/ai.html

- **Stanford Knowledge Systems Lab**
www-ksl.stanford.edu/

Arts

Galleries, art departments, and individual artists are featured here.

- **Agent 13**
agent13.com/

■ **Ankiewicz Studios**
www.ankiewicz.com

■ **Archives of American Art**
www.si.edu/organiza/offices/archart/
start.htm

■ **Art Crimes**
www.graffiti.org/

■ **Art Deco Erte**
www.ajarts.com/ajarts/

■ **Art of the First World War**
www.art-ww1.com/gb/index2.html

■ **Art of Tibet**
www.tibetart.com/

■ **ArtDaily**
www.artdaily.com/

■ **Arts Wire**
artswire.org/

■ **Asian Arts**
www.webart.com/asianart/index.html

■ **Babel**
www.babelny.com/

■ **Chicago Museum of
Contemporary Art**
www.mcachicago.org/

■ **Chihuly**
www.chihuly.com/

■ **Doubletake Gallery**
www.DoubletakeArt.com/

■ **Electric Art Gallery**
www.egallery.com/

■ **Explore the Renaissance**
www.learner.org/exhibits/renaissance/

■ **Favela**
www.favela.org/intro/main.html

■ **Gallery Online**
www.galleryonline.com/

■ **Hackett-Freedman Online Gallery**
www.realart.com/

■ **Hirshhorn Museum**
www.si.edu/organiza/museums/hirsh/

■ **Incredible Art Department**
www.artswire.org/kenroar/

■ **Kosmo**
www.akosmoproduction.com/

■ **Lounge Gallery of Art**
www.the-lounge.com/

■ **Martin Lawrence Galleries**
www.martinlawrence.com/

■ **Mundo das Artes**
www.interart.com.br/

■ **Musees de Paris**
www.paris.org/Musees/

■ **Museum of American Folk Art**
www.folkartmuse.org

■ **Museum of Bad Art**
glyphs.com/moba/

■ **National Gallery of Art**
www.nga.gov/

■ **New Chinese Art**
www.asiasociety.org/arts/insideout/

■ **On the Road in China**
www.zama.com/ontheroad/

■ **Orange Show**
www.insync.net/~orange/

■ **Portraits in Cyberspace**
persona.www.media.mit.edu/1010/Exhibit/

■ **Remedi Project**
www.theremediproject.com/

■ **Salvador Dali Collection**
www.webcoast.com/Dali/collection.htm

■ **SevenSeven**
www.sevenseven.com/

■ **Van Gogh Gallery**
www.vangoghgallery.com/

■ **Walker Art Center**
www.walkerart.org/

■ **Web Art**
www.mowa.org/

▲ www.mowa.org/

■ **Webbed Feats**
www.webbedfeats.org/

Astronomy

Mostly formal astronomy study.

- **American Astronomical Society**
www.aas.org/
- **Astronomy Café**
www2.ari.net/home/odenwald/cafe.html
- **Astronomy Picture of the Day**
antwrp.gsfc.nasa.gov/apod/astropix.html
- **AstroWeb Consortium**
www.cv.nrao.edu/fits/www/astroweb.html
- **Big Bear Solar Observatory**
sundog.caltech.edu/
- **Cambridge Astronomy**
www.ast.cam.ac.uk/
- **Comets and Meteor Showers**
medicine.wustl.edu/~kronkg/
- **Earth and Sky**
www.earthsky.com/
- **Earth Viewer**
www.fourmilab.ch/earthview/
vplanet.html
- **Griffith Observatory**
www.griffithobs.org/
- **Images of Galaxies**
zebu.uoregon.edu/galaxy.html
- **Inconstant Moon**
www.inconstantmoon.com/

■ **Should We Return to the Moon?**
www.ari.net/back2moon.html

■ **SKY Online**
www.skypub.com/

■ **United States Naval Observatory**
www.usno.navy.mil/

■ **University of Massachusetts Astronomy Department**
donald.phast.umass.edu/

■ **University of Toronto Astronomy Department**
lepus.astro.utoronto.ca/home.html

■ **University of Washington Astronomy Department**
www.astro.washington.edu/

■ **Web Nebulae**
seds.lpl.arizona.edu/billa/twn/top.html

■ **Windows to the Universe**
www.windows.umich.edu/

Auctions

Most of the sites listed here are for online auctions—list, sell, bid, and buy right from your computer at home. A few sites describe land-based auctions.

■ **Auction Depot**
www.auctiondepot.com/

- **Auction Guide**
www.auctionguide.com/index.htm

- **Auction Texas**
www.auction-tx.com/

- **Auction Track**
www.itrack.com/

- **Auction Universe**
www.auctionuniverse.com/

- **Auction Watch**
www.auctionwatch.com/

- **Auction! Auction!**
auctionauction.com/

- **AuctionBiz**
www.auctionbiz.com/

- **Auctiongoer's Guide**
www.auctiongoer.com/

- **BidNow**
www.bidnow.com/

- **Buffalo Bid Antique Auction**
www.buffalobid.com/

- **Buy Collectibles**
www.buycollectibles.com/

- **Christie's**
www.christies.com/

- **Collector Online**
www.collectoronline.com/

- **Cyberswap**
www.cyberswap.com/

■ **DealDeal**
www.dealdeal.com/

■ **eBay**
www.ebay.com/

■ **First Auction**
www.firstauction.com/

■ **France Auction Web**
www.auction-fr.com/index_uk.html

■ **Global Auction**
global-auction.com/

■ **Government Auction Listings**
www.govauctions.org/

■ **Haggle Online**
www.everyproduct.com/

■ **Interactive Collector**
www.icollector.com/

■ **Internet Auction List**
www.internetauctionlist.com/

■ **Online Auction**
www.online-auction.com/

■ **OnSale Computer Auction**
www.onsale.com/

■ **Pottery Auction**
www.potteryauction.com/

■ **Sotheby's**
www.sothebys.com/

■ **Sporting Auction**
www.sportingauction.com/

■ **Stardoodles Charity Auction**
www.stardoodle.com/index.shtml#movies

■ **uBid**
www.ubid.com/

Authors

Are all the "important" writers here? Alas, no matter who is on your list of important writers, the answer must be no. There is a site for an author only if someone has the desire and the ability to write it. Fortunately, many academics, the main source of these pages, have both.

■ **Sholom Aleichem**
www.sholom-aleichem.org/

■ **Maya Angelou**
www.cwrl.utexas.edu/~mmaynard/Maya/
maya5.html

■ **Isaac Asimov**
www.clark.net/pub/edseiler/WWW/
asimov_home_page.html

■ **Margaret Atwood**
www.web.net/owtoad/toc.html

■ **Jane Austen**
uts.cc.utexas.edu/~churchh/janeinfo.html

■ **Pearl S. Buck**
dept.english.upenn.edu/Projects/Buck/

■ **William S. Burroughs**
www.bigtable.com/

■ **Albert Camus**
www.sccs.swarthmore.edu/~pwillen1/lit/
indexa.htm

■ **Raymond Carver**
world.std.com/~ptc

■ **Willa Cather**
icg.harvard.edu/~cather/

■ **G. K. Chesterton**
www.chesterton.org/

■ **Arthur C. Clarke**
www.lsi.usp.br/~rbianchi/clarke

■ **Emily Dickinson**
www.planet.net/pkrisxle/emily/
dickinson.html

■ **E. L. Doctorow**
www.albany.edu/tree-tops/docs.
writers-inst/doctorow.html

■ **Umberto Eco**
www4.ncsu.edu/eos/users/m/mcmesser/
www/eco.html

■ **Louise Erdrich**
students.vcsu.nodak.edu/~toni_nelson/

■ **William Faulkner**
www.mcsr.olemiss.edu/~egjbp/faulkner/
faulkner.html

■ **F. Scott Fitzgerald**
www.pbs.org/kteh/amstorytellers/bios.html

■ **Charles Frazier**
www.sc.edu/library/spcoll/amlit/frazier/
frazier.html

■ **Dashiell Hammett**
www.mysterynet.com/history/hammett/

■ **Nathaniel Hawthorne**
eldred.ne.mediaone.net/nh/hawthorne.htm

■ **Joseph Heller**
www.levity.com/corduroy/heller.htm

■ **Ernest Hemingway**
www.ee.mcgill.ca/~nverever/hem/
pindex.html

■ **Hermann Hesse**
www.mcl.ucsb.edu/hesse/

■ **Zora Neale Hurston**
pages.prodigy.com/zora/

■ **Samuel Johnson**
www.ozemail.com.au/~reidb/

■ **James Joyce**
www.cohums.ohio-state.edu/english/
organizations/ijjf/

■ **Franz Kafka**
www.temple.edu/kafka/

■ **Jack Kerouac**
www.levity.com/corduroy/kerouac.htm

■ **Barbara Kingsolver**
www.kingsolver.com/

■ **Jack London**
sunsite.berkeley.edu/London/

■ **Thomas Mann**
mvmhp64.ciw.uni-
karlsruhe.de/tmg/tmpage. html

■ **Gabriel Garcia Marquez**
www.kirjasto.sci.fi/marquez.htm

■ **Herman Melville**
www.melville.org/

■ **John Milton**
www.mindspring.com/
~verax/milton.htm

■ **Toni Morrison**
www.viconet.com/~ejb/
intro.htm

▲ www.melville.org/

■ **Thomas Pynchon**
pete.pomona.edu/
pynchon/

■ **Anne Rice**
www.annerice.com/

■ **Tom Robbins**
www.rain.org/~da5e/tom_robbins.html

■ **John Steinbeck**
www.wwu.edu/~stephan/Steinbeck/
index.html

■ **August Strindberg**
www.extrapris.com/astrindberg.html

■ **Amy Tan**
www.luminarium.org/contemporary/
amytan/

■ **James Thurber**
www.seanet.com/~thurber/thurber.html

■ **J. R. R. Tolkien**
www.csclub.uwaterloo.ca/u/relipper/tolkien/
rootpage.html

■ **Mark Twain**
marktwain.miningco.com/

■ **John Updike**
www.users.fast.net/~joyerkes/

■ **Jules Verne**
www.math.technion.ac.il/~rl/JulesVerne/
biblio/

■ **Kurt Vonnegut**
www.duke.edu/~crh4/kv/kv.html

■ **Alice Walker**
www.luminarium.org/contemporary/alicew/

■ **Evelyn Waugh**
e2.empirenet.com/~jahvah/waugh/

■ **Rebecca Wells**
www.ya-ya.com/

■ **Eudora Welty**
www.anova.org/welty.html

■ **Walt Whitman**
memory.loc.gov/ammem/wwhome.html

■ **Tom Wolfe**
www.tomwolfe.com/

Aviation and Aerospace

A lot of hot stuff here, from private pilots to World War II to airline disasters.

■ **Aerospace Resources on the Internet**
www.cranfield.ac.uk/cils/library/subjects/airmenu.htm

■ **Air Affair**
www.airaffair.com/

▲ www.airaffair.com/

■ **Aircraft Owners and Pilots Association**
www.aopa.org/

■ **Airline History Archives**
www.flash.net/~airline/aha.html

■ **Airline History**
www.algonet.se/~hansj/history.htm

■ **AirNav**
www.airnav.com/

■ **Airshow.com**
www.airshow.com/

■ **Aviation Digest**
www.avdigest.com/default.html

■ **Be a Pilot**
www.beapilot.com/

■ **Canadian Snowbirds**
www.snowbirds.dnd.ca/

■ **Flights of Inspiration**
www.fi.edu/flights/

■ **Flying Tigers**
www2.gol.com/users/sychang/WB/

■ **Helicopter Association**
www.rotor.com/

■ **Instrumenting a Research Aircraft**
www.dfrc.nasa.gov/People/Shafer/files/
instr.html

■ **International Council of Airshows**
www.airshows.org/

■ **International Organization of Women Pilots**
www.ninety-nines.org/

■ **Major Airline Disasters**
dnausers.d-n-a.net/dnetGOjg/Disasters.htm

■ **National Soaring Museum**
www.soaringmuseum.org/

■ **Photovault's Aerospace and Aviation**
www.photovault.com/Link/Technology/AerospaceMaster.html

■ **Red Arrows**
www.deltaweb.co.uk/reds/redhome.htm

■ **San Diego Aerospace Museum**
www.aerospacemuseum.org/

■ **Scramble**
www.scramble.nl/

■ **Spitfire Is 60**
www.deltaweb.co.uk/spitfire/index.htm

■ **Student Pilot Network**
www.ufly.com/

■ **U.S. Fighter Squadrons**
www.unityproductions.com/usfs/index.html

■ **U.S. Wings Bomber Jackets**
www.pilotshops.com/

■ **Ultralight Flying Magazine**
www.ulflyingmag.com/

■ **United States Navy Blue Angels**
www.blueangels.navy.mil/

Award Givers

These sites evaluate other sites and hand out awards in the form of small graphics that can be

*displayed on winner sites. Good places to start the
hunt for quality sites.*

■ **Cool at Web**
www.web-search.com/cool.html

■ **Cyber-Teddy**
www.cyberteddy-online.com/

■ **High Five**
www.highfive.com/

■ **Lycos Top 5%**
point.lycos.com/categories/

■ **Magellan 4-Star**
www.mckinley.com

■ **Rubber Chicken**
rubberchicken.infospace.com/funsite.htm

■ **Studio ONE**
www.ippa.org/studio/studio.html

■ **Tech Sightings**
www.techsightings.com/

■ **Top 50 Sites That Download Quickly**
www.zazz.com/fast50/index.shtml

■ **USA Today Hot Site**
www.usatoday.com/life/cyber/ch.htm

Best, Hot, Cool

*Someone, somewhere has decided that the sites on
these lists are worth a look. They usually are.*

■ 25 Most Useful Sites
www3.zdnet.com/yil/content/depts/
useful/25mostuse.html

■ Best of the Web
botw.org/

■ Canadian Cool Site of the Week
www.escape.ca/~keir/cdncool/

■ Cool Central Site of the Day
www.coolcentral.com/day/

■ Cool Sightings
www.projectcool.com/sightings/

■ Cool Tool of the Day
www.cooltool.com/

■ Cybertown's Site of the Week
www.cybertown.com/spider.html

■ Daily Web Site
www.dailywebsite.com/

■ Dr. Webster
www.drwebster.com/

■ Dynamite Site of the Nite
www.netzone.com/~tti/dsotn.html

■ Family Site of the Day
www.worldvillage.com/famsite.htm

■ Internet Top Ten
www.chartshow.co.uk/

■ Lynx of the Week
web-star.com/lotw/lotw.html

■ **Project Cool Sightings**
www.projectcool.com/sightings/

■ **Too Cool**
www.toocool.com/

■ **Web Today Destinations**
www.web-today.net/webtoday/

■ **WELL-chosen Sites**
www.well.com/pointers.html

■ **Xplore Site of the Day**
www.xplore.com/xplore500/medium/
menu.html

Books and Reading

If you are the kind of person who must tear yourself away from a book to even look at this list, you will find further temptations here.

■ **1stBooks**
www.1stbooks.com/

■ **A Word a Day**
www.wordsmith.org/awad/index.html

■ **African American Literature**
aalbc.com/

■ **Afterhours Inspirational Stories**
inspirationalstories.com/

■ **Banned Books Week**
www.ala.org/bbooks/

■ **Books That Changed My Life**
www.well.com/user/woodman/books.html

■ **BookWeb**
www.ambook.org

■ **Candlelight Stories**
www.CandlelightStories.com/

■ **Chapter One**
www.washingtonpost.com/
wp-srv/style/books/features/chapone.htm

■ **Classic Short Stories**
www.bnl.com/shorts/

■ **Complete Works of Shakespeare**
the-tech.mit.edu/Shakespeare/works.html

■ **Concordances of Great Books**
www.concordance.com/

■ **Cybereditions**
cybereditions.com/

■ **Electronic Book and Text Sites**
www.awa.com/library/omnimedia/
links.html

■ **Electronic Text Center**
etext.lib.virginia.edu/uvaonline.html

■ **Fray**
www.fray.com/

■ **Future of the Book**
www.christopher.org/fob/index.html

■ **Internet Classics Archive**
classics.mit.edu/

- ■ **Luminarium**
  www.luminarium.org/lumina.htm
- ■ **Most Frequently Banned Books**
  www.cs.cmu.edu/People/spok/
  most-banned.html
- ■ **Online Literature Library**
  www.literature.org/Works/
- ■ **Printing Press as an Agent of Change**
  virtual.park.uga.edu/~hypertxt/eisenstein.html
- ■ **Project Gutenberg**
  www.promo.net/pg/
- ■ **Publishers Weekly Bestseller List**
  www.bookwire.com/PW/bsl/
  bestseller-index.html
- ■ **Serious Fiction**
  marylaine.com/bookbyte/serious.html

Business—Finance and Investing

The financial community has figured out that many regular Internet users are also investors—or would like to be. Accordingly, many attractive sites promote their wares.

- ■ **Armchair Millionaire**
  www.armchairmillionaire.com/

■ **Bank of America**
www.BankAmerica.com/

■ **Bloomberg Personal**
www.bloomberg.com/

■ **Charles Schwab**
www.schwab.com/

■ **Day Traders**
www.daytraders.com/

■ **Dogs of the Dow**
www.dogsofthedow.com/

■ **Final Bell**
www.sandbox.net/finalbell/pub-doc/
home. html

■ **Free Stock Quotes**
www.freerealtime.com/

■ **International Monetary Fund**
www.imf.org/

■ **Investor Links**
www.investorlinks.com/

■ **Message Media**
www.messagemedia.com/

■ **Money Advisor**
www.moneyadvisor.com/

■ **Motley Fool**
www.fool.com/

■ **Nasdaq**
www.nasdaq.com/

■ **New York Stock Exchange**
www.nyse.com/

■ **Silicon Investor**
www.techstocks.com/

■ **Standard and Poor**
www.stockinfo.standardpoor.com/

■ **Stock Club**
stockclub.com/

■ **Stock Smart**
www.stocksmart.com/

■ **StockMaster**
www.stockmaster.com/

▲ www.stockclub.com/

■ **StreetEYE Index**
www.streeteye.com/

■ **Wells Fargo**
www.wellsfargo.com/

■ **World Bank**
www.worldbank.org/

■ **Worldly Investor**
www.worldlyinvestor.com/

■ **Young Investor**
www.younginvestor.com/

Business—General

This list is a potpourri of several aspects of business. For pure entertainment, and even nostalgia, don't miss the 50 Best Commercials.

■ **50 Best Commercials**
adage.com/news_and_features/
special_reports/commercials

■ **Advertising Age**
www.adage.com/

■ **Better Business Bureau**
www.bbbonline.org

■ **BidCast**
www.bidcast.com/

■ **Big Book**
www.bigbook.com/

■ **Business Video**
www.businessvideo.msnbc.com

■ **BusinessSeek**
www.businesseek.com

■ **CardWeb**
www.ramresearch.com/

■ **Companies Online Search**
www.companiesonline.com/

■ **Company Sleuth**
www.companysleuth.com/

■ **Dow Jones Business Directory**
businessdirectory.dowjones.com/

■ **Executive PayWatch**
www.paywatch.org/

■ **Forbes**
www.forbes.com/

■ **Fortune 500**
cgi.pathfinder.com/fortune/fortune500/
index.html

■ **Franchise Info**
www.frannet.com/

■ **Industry Net**
www.industry.net

■ **Industry Week**
www.industryweek.com/

■ **InfoUSA**
www.lookupusa.com/

■ **ITEX Barter**
www.tradebanc.com/

■ **NewsPage**
www.newspage.com/

■ **Nightly Business Report**
www.nightlybusiness.org

■ **Researching Companies on
the Internet**
home.sprintmail.com/~debflanagan/

■ **Smart Business Supersite**
www.smartbiz.com/

■ **Wharton Business Knowledge**
knowledge.wharton.upenn.edu/

Calendars

Fun and perhaps an occasional necessity.

■ **Algebra: Fun with Calendars**
math.rice.edu/~lanius/Lessons/calen.html

■ **American Secular
Holidays Calendar**
www.smart.net/~mmontes/ushols.html

■ **Ancient Calendars**
physics.nist.gov/GenInt/Time/ancient.html

■ **Calendar FAQs**
www.pip.dknet.dk/~pip10160/calendar.html

■ **Calendar Zone**
www.calendarzone.com/

■ **Chinese Calendar**
www.cnd.org/Other/calendar.html

■ **Famous Birthdays**
www.famousbirthdays.com/

■ **International Elections Calendar**
www.klipsan.com/calendar.htm

■ **One-World Global Calendar**
www.zapcom.net/phoenix.arabeth/
1world.html

■ **Phases of the Moon**
www.lunaroutreach.org/phases/phases.cgi

Career/Jobs

*Not all here will suit you, but all are worth a look.
See also* Resume Services.

■ **4Work**
www.4work.com/

■ **America's Job Bank**
www.ajb.dni.us/index.html

■ **Ask the Headhunter**
www.asktheheadhunter.com/

■ **Best Jobs USA**
www.bestjobsusa.com/

■ **Brave New Work World**
www.newwork.com/

■ **C++ Jobs**
www.cplusplusjobs.com/

■ **Career Central**
www.careercentral.com/index.asp

■ **Career City**
www.careercity.com/

■ **Career Exposure**
www.careerexposure.com/index2.html

■ **Career Internetworking**
www.careerkey.com/

■ **Career Resource Center**
www.careers.org/

■ **Career.com**
www.career.com/

■ **CareerBuilder Network**
www.careerbuilder.com/

■ **CareerMosaic**
www.careermosaic.com/

■ **CareerPath**
careerpath.com/

■ **CareerPro**
www.career-pro.com/index.htm

■ **CareerWeb**
www.careerweb.com/

■ **Computer Programming Jobs**
www.developers.net/

■ **ComputerJobs**
www.computerjobs.com/

■ **ComputerWork**
www.computerwork.com/

■ **Digital Station**
www.digitalstation.com/

■ **Eagleview**
www.eagleview.com/

■ **Employease**
www.employease.com/

■ **Entry Level Job Seeker Assistant**
members.aol.com/Dylander/jobhome.html

■ **Fee Free Jobs and Resumes**
www.feefree.com/

■ **First Steps in the Hunt**
www.interbiznet.com/hunt/

■ **GetWork Network**
www.getwork.net/

■ **HeadHunter**
www.headhunter.net/

■ **Help-Wanted Page**
www.helpwantedpage.com/

■ **High Technology Careers Magazine**
www.hightechcareers.com/

■ **High-Tech Career Fairs**
www.cfcjobs.com/

■ **HotJobs 2000**
www.hotjobs2000.com/

■ **HotJobs**
www.hotjobs.com/

■ **Java Jobs Online**
javajobs.com/

■ **Job Doctor**
www.thejobdr.com/

■ **Job Resource**
www.thejobresource.com/

■ **Job Search Services**
www.job-searcher.com/

■ **JobDirect**
www.jobdirect.com/

■ **JobEngine**
www.jobengine.com/

■ **JobHunt**
www.job-hunt.org/resume.shtml

■ **JobOptions**
www.joboptions.com

■ **Jobs by State**
www.coolworks.com/showme/state.htm

■ **Jobs Online**
www.jobs-online.net/

■ **JobSafari**
www.jobsafari.com/

■ **Jobtrak**
www.jobtrak.com/

■ **JobWeb**
www.jobweb.org/

■ **Monster Board**
www.monster.com/

■ **National Job Bank**
www.nlbbs.com/~najoban/

■ **NationJob**
www.nationjob.com/

■ **NetJobs Canada**
www.netjobs.com

■ **Resumail**
www.resumail.com/

■ **Select Jobs**
www.selectjobs.com

■ **Software Jobs**
www.softwarejobs.com/

■ **Summer Jobs**
www.summerjobs.com/

■ **Tech Jobs Supersite**
supersite.net/techjobs/

■ **TechNet**
www.techemployment.com/

■ **TechSearch**
www.jobsight.com/

■ **Telecommuting Jobs**
www.tjobs.com/

■ **Temp 24-7**
www.temp24-7.com/

■ **TV Jobs**
www.tvjobs.com/

■ **Vault Job Board**
www.vaultreports.com/resume/post2/
post.cfm

■ **Virtual Job Fair**
www.vjf.com/

■ **Web Jobs USA**
www.webjobsusa.com/

Cars and Trucks

You can get advice or check out parts or even kick the tires of a new car. Or buy one.

■ **American Automobile Association**
www.aaa.com/

■ **Auto Mall USA**
www.automallusa.com/

■ **Auto Web**
www.autoweb.com

■ **AutoConnect**
autoconnect.com/

■ **Automobile Leasing**
www.mindspring.com/~ahearn/lease/
lease.html

■ **Automotive Site of Excellence**
www.4x44u.com/pub/k2/ase.htm

■ **Autopedia**
www.autopedia.com/

■ **Autorama**
autorama.com/

■ **Autorow**
www.autorow.com/

■ **AutoSite**
www.autosite.com/

■ **Car Center**
www.intellichoice.com/

■ **Car Connection**
www.thecarconnection.com/

■ **Car Place**
www.thecarplace.com/

■ **Car Recalls**
www.nhtsa.dot.gov/cars/problems/

■ **Car Stuff**
www.automallusa.com/cgi-bin/index2.cgi

■ **Car Tracker**
www.cartrackers.com/

■ **CarPoint**
carpoint.msn.com/

■ **Cartalk**
www.cartalk.com/

■ **Classic Cars**
www.classicar.com/museums/aacalbry/
aacalbry.htm

■ **Crash Tests**
www.crashtest.com/intro/index.htm

■ **IntelliChoice Car Center**
www.carpoint.msn.com/

■ **J. D. Power and Associates**
www.jdpower.com/press.html

■ **Kelley Blue Book**
www.kbb.com/index.html

■ **Land Rover**
www.landrover.com/

■ **Motor Trend**
www.motortrend.com/

■ **NASCAR Online**
www.nascar.com/

■ **No Risk Used Car Buying**
www.goodasnew.com/

■ **Popular Mechanics**
popularmechanics.com/

■ **Special Cars**
www.specialcar.com/

■ **Virtual Auto Parts Store**
gate.cruzio.com/~vaps/

■ **Weekend Mechanics Club**
www.weekendmechanicsclub.com/

Cities

Many of these U.S. city sites emphasize the official arm of the government; others focus on tourism.

■ **Albuquerque**
www.albuquerque.com/

■ **Anaheim**
anaheim.areaguides.net/

■ **Annapolis**
www.capitalonline.com/tour/

■ **Anchorage**
www.alaska.net/~acvb/

■ **Arlington**
www.ci.arlington.tx.us/

■ **Atlanta**
www.atlanta.org/

■ **Atlantic City**
www.virtualac.com/

■ **Aurora**
aurora.areaguides.net/

■ **Austin**
austin.citysearch.com/

■ **Baltimore**
baltimore.areaguides.net/

■ **Birmingham**
birmingham.areaguides.net/

■ **Boise**
www.ci.boise.id.us/

■ **Boston**
www.ci.boston.ma.us/

■ **Buffalo**
buffalo.areaguides.net/

■ **Charlotte**
charlotte.areaguides.net/

■ **Chicago**
www.centerstage.net/chicago/

■ **Cincinnati**
www.cincinnati.com/

■ **Cleveland**
www.cleveland.com/

■ **Colorado Springs**
www.csurf.com/csurf/tour.html

■ **Columbus**
www.ci.columbus.oh.us/

■ **Corpus Christi**
corpuschristi.areaguides.net/

■ **Dallas**
www.ci.dallas.tx.us/

■ **Denver**
www.denver.org/

■ **Detroit**
www.ci.detroit.mi.us/

- **El Paso**
elpaso.areaguides.net/
- **Fairbanks**
www.areaguide.net/fairbanks
- **Fort Worth**
www.fortworth.acn.net/
- **Fresno**
www.ci.fresno.ca.us/
- **Gainesville**
www.state.fl.us/gvl/
- **Hartford**
www.hartford.com/
- **Honolulu**
www.co.honolulu.hi.us/
- **Houston**
www.ci.houston.tx.us
- **Indianapolis**
www.indplsconnect.com/
- **Jacksonville**
www.ci.jax.fl.us/
- **Kansas City**
www.kcmo.org/
- **Las Vegas**
www.lasvegas.org/
- **Lexington**
lexington.areaguides.net/
- **Little Rock**
www.littlerock.com/

- **Long Beach**
www.ci.long-beach.ca.us/

- **Los Angeles**
www.ci.la.ca.us/

- **Louisville**
www.louisville-visitors.com/

- **Memphis**
www.ci.memphis.tn.us/

- **Mesa**
www.ci.mesa.az.us/

- **Miami**
www.miami.com/

- **Milwaukee**
www.ci.mil.wi.us/

- **Minneapolis**
www.citypages.com/

- **Nashville**
nashville.citysearch.com/

- **New Orleans**
www.noconnect.com/

- **New York**
ny.state.org/nyc/tourism/

- **Newark**
newark.areaguides.net/

- **Oakland**
oakland.areaguides.net/

- **Oklahoma City**
oklahomacity.areaguides.net/

■ **Omaha**
www.ci.omaha.ne.us/

■ **Philadelphia**
www.gophila.com/

■ **Phoenix**
www.ci.phoenix.az.us/

■ **Pittsburgh**
www.pittsburgh.net/

■ **Portland**
www.ci.portland.or.us/

■ **Raleigh**
www.raleigh-nc.org/

■ **Reno**
www.reno.com/

■ **Riverside**
www.ci.riverside.ca.us/

■ **Sacramento**
sacramento.areaguides.net/

■ **Salt Lake City**
www.ci.slc.ut.us/

■ **San Antonio**
www.sachamber.com/Tourism.htm

■ **San Diego**
www.seesandiego.com/

■ **San Francisco**
sanfrancisco.citysearch.com/

■ **San Jose**
www.sanjose.org/nsapi/sj_home_page

■ **Santa Ana**
www.santaanacc.com/search1.htm

■ **Santa Fe**
www.santafe.org/

■ **Santa Monica**
pen.ci.santa-monica.ca.us/

■ **Savannah**
www.savannah-online.com/

■ **Seattle**
www.pan.ci.seattle.wa.us/

■ **Shreveport**
www.ci.shreveport.la.us/

■ **St. Louis**
stlouis.areaguides.net/

■ **St. Paul**
stpaul.areaguides.net/

■ **St. Petersburg**
stpete.org/

■ **Syracuse**
www.syracuse.com/

■ **Tallahassee**
www.tallahassee.com/

■ **Tampa**
tampa.areaguides.net/

■ **Toledo**
www.ci.toledo.oh.us/Homepage.html

■ **Tucson**
www.ci.tucson.az.us/

■ **Tulsa**
www.ci.tulsa.ok.us/

■ **Virginia Beach**
virginiabeach.areaguides.net/

■ **Washington, D.C.**
www.washington.org/

■ **Wichita**
www.wichita.com/

College

Most college sites represent a specific school; you can find yours by using a search engine. Generic college-related sites are listed here.

■ **Admissions Information**
www.collegexpress.com/admissions/
index.html

■ **Adults Back to College**
www.back2college.com/

■ **All About College**
www.allaboutcollege.com/

■ **All Campus In-Sites**
www.allcampus.com/

■ **American Universities**
www.planet-hawaii.com/global/
universy.html

■ **Be Real, Get In**
www.jayi.com/ACG/articles/Be_Real.html

■ **Business Schools**
ulinks.com/list/business.html

■ **Campus Tours**
www.campustours.com/

■ **College Choice Website**
www.gseis.ucla.edu/mm/cc/home.html

■ **College Edge**
www.collegeedge.com/

■ **College Home Pages**
www.mit.edu:8001/people/cdemello/
univ.html

■ **Community College Web**
www.mcli.dist.maricopa.edu/cc/

■ **CyberCampus**
www.cybercampus.com/

■ **Dormitories Around the World**
www.heim1.tu-clausthal.de/
studentenwohnheime/english/

■ **Gradschools.com**
www.gradschools.com/

■ **Main Quad**
www.mainquad.com/

■ **Peterson's Education Supersite**
www.petersons.com/

■ **Security on Campus**
campussafety.org/

■ **Student Political Network**
www.cis.yale.edu/ypunion/ASPN.html

■ **Study Abroad**
www.nrcsa.com/

■ **Study Abroad Directory**
www.studyabroad.com./

■ **United States Student Association**
www.essential.org/ussa/ussa.html

■ **Virtual Dorm**
www.vdorm.com/new/

■ **Western Governors University**
www.wgu.edu/wgu/index.html

Computer History

Several people give us details, sometimes from their personal experiences, about how it all started. See also Internet History.

■ **Charles Babbage Institute**
www.cbi.umn.edu/

■ **Chronology of Events in the History of Microcomputers**
www3.islandnet.com/~kpolsson/comphist.htm

■ **Computer Chronicles: From Stone to Silicon**
despina.advanced.org/22522/

■ **Computer Museum**
www.tcm.org/

■ **Digital Moments**
www.menuez.com/

■ **First Virtual Mousepad Museum**
www.expa.hvu.nl/ajvdhek/

■ **Historical Computer Society**
www.cyberstreet.com/hcs/hcs.htm

■ **History of Computing**
ei.cs.vt.edu/~history/index.html

■ **History of Shareware**
www.pslweb.com/history.htm

■ **History of the Apple Computer**
www.apple-history.com/

■ **IEEE Annals of the History of Computing**
www.computer.org/annals/

■ **Macintosh Museum**
www.macintoshos.com/macintosh.museum/
index.shtml

■ **Memoir: Homebrew Computer Club**
www.bambi.net/bob/homebrew.html

■ **Mind Machine Museum**
userwww.sfsu.edu/~hl/mmm.html

■ **MouseSite**
sloan.stanford.edu/MouseSite/

■ **Obsolete Computer Museum**
www.ncsc.dni.us/fun/user/tcc/cmuseum/
cmuseum.htm

■ **Silicon Valley History and Future**
www.internetvalley.com/introduction.html

■ **Silicon Valley History**
www.silvalonline.com/silhist.html

■ **Smithsonian Computer History**
www.si.edu/resource/tours/comphist/
computer.htm

■ **Software History Center**
www.softwarehistory.org/

■ **Tech Museum of Innovation**
www.thetech.org/

■ **The Machine That Changed the World**
ei.cs.vt.edu/~history/TMTCTW.html

■ **The Revolutionaries**
www.thetech.org/revolutionaries/

■ **Univac Memories**
www.fourmilab.ch/documents/univac/
index.html

■ **Virtual Computer History Museum**
video.cs.vt.edu:90/history/

Computer Organizations and Events

If you want to join, go to the convention, or just figure out who these people are, check out their sites.

■ **ACM Association of Computing Machinery**
info.acm.org

■ **AITP Association of Information Technology Professionals**
www.dpmalv.org/

■ **Association of Internet Professionals**
www.association.org

■ **AWC Association for Women in Computing**
www.awc-hq.org/

■ **Comdex**
www.comdex.com/

■ **ICCA Independent Computer Consultants Association**
www.icca.org/

■ **ICCP Institute for Certification of Computer Professionals**
www.iccp.org/

■ **IEEE Computer Society**
www.computer.org/

■ **Internet Conference Calendar**
conferences.calendar.com/index.shtml

■ **TechCalendar**
www.techweb.com/calendar/

Computer Science

Sites of interest to computer science people, especially those related to the Internet, are spread throughout this book. This list mentions a few topics more specific to the field.

- **Advanced Computing Laboratory**
www.acl.lanl.gov/

- **Bell Labs Library**
www.bell-labs.com/bllib.html

- **Center for Information Technology**
logic.stanford.edu/cit/

- **Computer Science Journals**
fas.sfu.ca/1/projects/ElectronicLibrary/
Collections/CMPT/csjournals/

- **Computing Dictionary**
www.InstantWeb.com/foldoc/

- **Diccionario—Terminos Informaticos**
www.ctv.es/USERS/angelaj/

- **Glossary of Computer Abbreviations**
www.access.digex.net/~ikind/babel.html

- **IEEE Standards**
standards.ieee.org/

- **Internet Parallel Computing Archive**
www.hensa.ac.uk/parallel/

- **LinuxWorld**
www.linuxworld.com/

- **Microsoft Research**
www.research.microsoft.com/

■ **MIT Media Lab**
www.media.mit.edu/

■ **National Center for Supercomputing Applications**
www.ncsa.uiuc.edu/

■ **Online Computing Journals**
www.utexas.edu/computer/vcl/journals.html

■ **Soft Center**
www.softcenter.se/

■ **Sony Computer Science Lab**
www.csl.sony.co.jp/

■ **Technology Transfer Virtual Library**
www.nttc.edu/gov/other/tech.html

■ **U.S. Computer Science Departments**
www.utexas.edu/computer/vcl/acadcomp.html

■ **UNC MetaLab**
metalab.unc.edu/splash.html

■ **Unix Guru Universe**
www.ugu.com/

■ **World Lecture Hall**
www.utexas.edu/world/lecture/cs/

Computers—Programming and Languages

A small collection of sites. See also Java *and* Home Page—HTML Help Sites.

■ **Ask the SQL Pro**
www.inquiry.com/techtips/thesqlpro/

■ **Ask the Visual Basic Pro**
www.inquiry.com/thevbpro/

■ **C++ Report**
www.creport.com/

■ **C++ Web Site**
www.topcode.com/c++/main.shtml

■ **Carl and Gary's Visual Basic Home Page**
www.cgvb.com/

■ **CGI Resource Index**
www.cgi-resources.com/

■ **Computer Programming Languages**
src.doc.ic.ac.uk/bySubject/Computing/
Languages.html

■ **From the Ground Up: A Guide to C++**
library.advanced.org/3074/

■ **Game Design 101**
www.gamecenter.com/Features/Exclusives/
Design/

■ **Game Programming Megasite**
www.perplexed.com/GPMega/

■ **IBM COBOL**
www.software.ibm.com/ad/cobol/

■ **Inside Visual Basic for Windows**
www.cobb.com/ivb/index.htm

■ **Introduction to C Programming**
devcentral.iftech.com/learning/tutorials/

■ **Object Oriented
Information Sources**
cuiwww.unige.ch/OSG/OOinfo/

■ **Object Oriented Software**
www.soft-design.com/softinfo/sdc.html

■ **Open Source Software**
public.resource.org/

■ **Programmer's Source**
www.progsource.com/index.html

■ **QBasic**
www.qbasic.com/

■ **WWW Virtual Library—
Software Engineering**
rbse.jsc.nasa.gov/virt-lib/soft-eng.html

Cool Companies

*Know them by their cool sites. Several of these sites
have multimedia features.*

■ **American Express**
www6.americanexpress.com/travel/
index.html

■ **Ben and Jerry's Ice Cream**
www.benjerry.com/

- **Boeing**
www.boeing.com/
- **Bristol-Myers Squibb**
www.bristolmyers.com/
- **Campbell Soup**
www.campbellsoup.com/
- **Caterpillar**
www.caterpillar.com/
- **Charles Schwab**
www.schwab.com/
- **Clark Bar**
www.clarkbar.com/
- **Colgate-Palmolive**
www.colgate.com/
- **ConAgra**
www.conagra.com/
- **Crayola**
www.crayola.com/
- **Disney**
www.disney.com/
- **Dunlop Tires**
www.dunloptire.com/
- **DuPont**
www.dupont.com/
- **E*Trade**
www.etrade.com/
- **Eastman Kodak**
www.kodak.com/

- **Eli Lilly**
www.elililly.com/
- **Esprit**
www.esprit.com/
- **FAO Schwarz**
www.faoschwarz.com/
- **Federal Express**
www.fedex.com/
- **Ferrari**
www.ferrari.it
- **Fila**
www.fila.com/
- **Ford**
www2.ford.com/
- **GTE**
www.gte.com/
- **HBO**
www.hbo.com/
- **Gatorade**
www.gatorade.com/
- **General Electric**
www.ge.com/
- **Gillette**
www.gillette.com/
- **Hershey**
www.hersheys.com/
- **Home Depot**
www.homedepot.com/

- **Honda**
www.honda.com/

- **Iams**
www.iams.com/

- **J. P. Morgan**
www.jpmorgan.com/

- **Johnson & Johnson**
www.johnsonjohnson.com/

- **Kellogg's**
www.kelloggs.com/index_cc.html

- **Kmart**
www.kmart.com/

- **Kraft**
www.kraftfoods.com/

- **Levi Strauss Jeans**
www.levi.com/

- **McDonalds**
www.mcdonalds.com/

- **MCI WorldCom**
www.mciworldcom.com/

- **Merck**
www.merck.com/

- **Mobil**
www.mobil.com/

- **Nestle**
www.nestle.com/

- **Nordstrom**
www.nordstrom.com/

■ **Office Depot**
www.officedepot.com/

■ **OfficeMax**
www.officemax.com/

■ **Pepsi**
www.pepsiworld.com/index2.html

■ **Pfizer**
www.pfizer.com/

■ **Polaroid**
www.polaroid.com/

■ **Saatchi and Saatchi**
www.saatchi-saatchi.com/

■ **Sears**
www.sears.com/

■ **Sharp Electronics**
www.sharp-usa.com/

■ **Starbucks**
www.starbucks.com/home.asp

■ **Taco Time**
www.tacotime.com/

■ **Tide ClothesLine**
www.clothesline.com/

■ **UPS**
www.ups.com

■ **Volkswagen**
www3.vw.com/
index4.htm

■ **Xerox**
www.xerox.com/

▲ www.ups.com

Consumer Information

If you never knew there were so many things to worry about, you will after you peruse this list and some of the sites.

■ **All You Can Eat**
www.foodnews.org/

■ **Appliance**
www.appliance.com/

■ **Cancel-It**
www.cancel-it.com/

■ **Choosing a Mover**
www.amconf.org/

■ **Consumer Handbook**
www.pueblo.gsa.gov/crh/respref.htm

■ **Consumer Information Center**
www.pueblo.gsa.gov/

■ **Consumer Law**
consumer.findlaw.com/

■ **Consumer Product Safety Commission**
www.cpsc.gov

■ **Consumer Protection**
www.wmbakerassociates.com/consprotect.html

■ **Consumer World**
www.consumerworld.org/

■ **Consumers Digest Online**
www.consumersdigest.com/

■ **Food Safety**
www.foodsafety.org/consumer.htm

■ **Home Inspection FAQs**
www.creia.com/faq.htm

■ **Insurance Company Ratings**
www.insure.com/ratings/index.html

■ **Pyramid Schemes and Chain Letters**
dcn.davis.ca.us/~btcarrol/skeptic/
pyramid.html

■ **Retail Sales Ploys**
www.bookouts.com/snake.htm

■ **Scambusters**
www.scambusters.org/

■ **Smart Consumer**
www.worth.com/articles/PC0.html

■ **Stop the Junk Mail**
www.stopjunk.com/

■ **Street Cents**
www.halifax.cbc.ca/streetcents/

Counting

We do a lot of counting on the Internet. And, for some reason, the favorite number is 100.

■ **100 Black Men of America**
www.charweb.org/organizations/
nonprofits/100bm/index100.htm

Counting

■ **100 High-Tech Career Fairs**
www.network-events.com/

■ **100 Hot Web Sites**
www.100hot.com/

■ **100 Largest Foreign Investments in the U.S.**
www.ofii.org/newsroom/news/forchart.html

■ **100 Largest U.S. Banks**
www.moneypage.com/pulse/cont100.htm

■ **100 Largest U.S. Cities**
www.amcity.com/journals/demographics/report57/57-1.html

■ **100 Photojournalists Cover One Digital Day**
www.veronica.nl/top100/

■ **100 Poems by 100 Poets**
vh1.com/special/100greatest/

■ **100 Recettes Bistro**
photo.net/wtr/100-things.html

■ **100 Things to Make Your Web Site Better**
photo.net/wtr/100-things.html

■ **100 Years of Horror Films**
www.aentv.com/home/horror/horrormain.htm

■ **100 Years of Radio**
www.alpcom.it/hamradio/evitto.html

■ **Billboard Hot 100**
www.billboard.com/charts/hot100.asp

■ **Canada Top 100 Sites**
www.canadatop100.com/

■ **Daily 100**
www.80s.com/Entertainment/Movies/
Daily100/

■ **Film 100**
www.film100.com/

■ **PC Magazine's Top 100**
www8.zdnet.com/pcmag/special/
web100/_open.htm

■ **The Shopping 100**
www.shopping100.com/

■ **Time 100: Artists and Entertainers**
cgi.pathfinder.com/time/time100/index.html

■ **Top 100 Brain Structures**
www.med.harvard.edu/AANLIB/cases/caseM/
case.html

■ **Top 100 Computer Magazines**
www.internetvalley.com/top100mag.html

■ **Top 100 High School
Football Prospects**
tamurecruiting.myriad.net/nat100.htm#list

■ **Top 100 Hospitals**
www2.hcia.com/100top/98/

■ **Top 100 Party Songs of All Time**
members.aol.com/yourparty/articles/ptyhit.htm

■ **Top 100 Posters**
www.allwall.com/asp/Top100-asp/_/
NV--1_F1/1.asp

■ **Top 100 Screen Savers**
www.top100screensavers.com/

■ **Top 100 TV Shows of All Time**
www.ultimatetv.com/news/top100/
top100.html

■ **Veronica Top 100 Countdown**
www.veronica.nl/top100/

■ **VH1 100 Great Artists**
vh1.com/special/100greatest/

■ **Web 100**
www.web100.com/

■ **Web Shopping 100**
www.shopping100.com/

■ **Wisecat's Top 100**
wisecat.co.uk/

■ **World's 100 Most Endangered Sites**
www.worldmonuments.org/list.html

Cycling

Touring, racing, commuting, or just out for an afternoon spin? It's all here on the Internet.

■ **Aardvark Cycles**
www.aardvarkcycles.com/

■ **Bicyclemasterpieces**
www.electriciti.com/gary/

■ **Bicycles on the Web**
www.cis.upenn.edu/~vinson/cycling.html

■ **Bicycling's Skill Center**
www.bicyclingmagazine.com/skill/

■ **Bike Club Directory**
www.adventuresports.com/asap/bike/
bikeclub.htm

■ **Bike Culture Quarterly**
bikeculture.com/home/

■ **Bike Current**
web2.thesphere.com/bikecurrent/

■ **Bike Ride Online**
www.bikeride.com/

■ **BikeSite**
bikesite.com/

■ **Club Tread Reports**
www.bltg.com/ctreport/index.htp

■ **Cyber Cyclery**
jones.nas.com/

■ **Le Tour de France**
www.letour.fr/

■ **Mountain Biking**
xenon.stanford.edu/~rsf/mtn-bike.html

■ **National Bicycle Greenway**
www.bikeroute.com/

■ **Project New Zealand**
www.projectnz.org/

■ **Science of Cycling**
www.exploratorium.edu/cycling/

■ **Specialized**
www.specialized.com/

■ **Stolen Bike Registry**
www.telalink.net/cycling/stolen.html

■ **Tailwinds**
www.voyager.net/tailwinds/

■ **Trek Bikes**
www.trekbikes.com/

■ **Unicycling**
ecstasy.winternet.com/usa/

■ **Velo Pages**
www.velopages.ch/

■ **VeloNews**
www.greatoutdoors.com/velonews/

■ **WWW Bicycle Lane**
www.bikelane.com/

Don'tcha Just Love It?

*There is nothing we can add to a description of
these sites that their titles don't already tell.*

■ **Antsite**
www.gizmonics.com/

■ **Asylum**
asylum.cid.com/

■ **Band-Aids**
www.savetz.com/bandaid/

■ **Carousels**
www.carousel.org/

■ **Carrot Top**
www.carrottop.com/

■ **Casbah**
www.dsiegel.com/

■ **Cyrano Love Letters**
www.nando.net/toys/cyrano.html

■ **DearMom**
www.dearmom.com/

■ **Famous Last Words**
web.mit.edu/randy/www/words.html

■ **Fractal Cow Studio**
www.fractalcow.com/

■ **Joe Boxer**
www.joeboxer.com/

■ **Kaleidoscopes**
www.ux1.eiu.edu/~csbdb/kr.html

■ **Miss Abigail's Time Warp Advice**
www.kreative.net/timewarp/

■ **The Box**
www.sixsides.com/

Electronic Commerce

Lots of help is available to both fledgling and established e-commerce merchants, as well as their customers.

■ **3 Steps to E-Commerce Success**
www.e-commerce1.com/

■ **BidCast**
www.bidcast.com/

■ **BizBot: Online Business Directory**
www.bizbot.org/

■ **Clue to Internet Commerce**
www.ppn.org/clue

■ **CyberCash**
www.cybercash.com/

■ **Cybersmarts**
www.ftc.gov/bcp/conline/pubs/online/
cybrsmrt.htm

■ **E Business**
www.hp.com/Ebusiness/main1.html

■ **E-Commerce Advisory Council**
www.e-commerce.ca.gov/

■ **E-Commerce News**
www.internetnews.com/ec-news/

■ **E-Commerce Times**
www.ecommercetimes.com/

■ **E-Commerce Treasure Trove**
www.wilsonweb.com/commerce/

■ **E-Commerce Exchange**
www.eccx.com/

■ **E-Commerce Guide**
ecommerce.internet.com/

■ **E-Commerce Resources**
www.acumen-solutions.co.uk/ecommerce/
resource.htm

■ **eWallet**
www.ewallet.com/

■ **Federal E-Commerce Program**
ec.fed.gov/

■ **ICAT Commerce Online**
www.icat.com/

■ **Internet Tax Freedom Act**
www.house.gov/chriscox/nettax/

■ **Jumbostore**
www.jumbostore.com/

■ **Link Exchange**
www.linkexchange.com/welcome/

■ **Public Eye**
www.thepubliceye.com/

■ **StoreFront**
www.storefront99.com/

■ **TRUSTe Directory**
www.truste.com/

■ **Upside Online**
www.upside.com/

■ **Web Marketing Today**
www.wilsonweb.com/wmt/

Economics

If you are an economist, an economist in training, or just a bystander who wonders how the economy runs, it's all here for the taking.

■ **Beige Book: Current Economic Conditions**
www.bog.frb.fed.us/FOMC/BeigeBook/Current/

■ **Brookings: Economic Studies**
www.brook.edu/ES/ES_HP.HTM

■ **Bureau of Economic Analysis**
www.bea.doc.gov/

■ **Bureau of National Affairs**
www.bna.com/

■ **Cato Institute**
www.cato.org/

■ **Dismal Scientist**
www.dismal.com/

■ **Econometrics Laboratory**
elsa.berkeley.edu/eml/

■ **Economic Analysis**
www.bea.doc.gov/

■ **Economic Research Service**
www.econ.ag.gov/

■ **Economic Statistics Briefing**
www.whitehouse.gov/fsbr/esbr.html

■ **Economic Time Series**
www.economagic.com/

■ **Economics Working Paper Archive**
econwpa.wustl.edu/

■ **Economy at a Glance**
stats.bls.gov/eag.table.html

■ **Federal Budget**
www.whitehouse.gov/OMB/budget/
index.html

■ **Federal Government Spending**
www.fedmoney.com/fedspending2.html

■ **FinWeb**
www.finweb.com/

■ **Foundation for Teaching Economics**
www.fte.org/

■ **IMF World Economic Outlook**
www.imf.org/external/pubs/ft/weo/1999/01/
index.htm

■ **Inflation Calculator**
www.westegg.com/inflation/

■ **Institute for
International Economics**
www.iie.com/

■ **Interactive Economic
Development Network**
iedn.com/IEDNonline/

■ **Internet Resources for Economists**
econwpa.wustl.edu/EconFAQ/EconFAQ.
html

■ **National Bureau of
Economic Research**
www.nber.org/

■ **RAND Journal of Economics**
www.rje.org/

■ **The Economist**
www.economist.com/

■ **The Great Depression**
www.scruz.net/~kangaroo/
THE_GREAT_DEPRESSION.htm

■ **Virtual Library in Economics**
www.hkkk.fi/EconVLib.html/

■ **WebEc**
www.helsinki.fi/WebEc/

Education

*Educators were early users of the Internet and
their contributions continue to be significant.
There is a rich trove of educational materials on
the Internet for current and future educators.*

■ **21st Century Teachers Network**
www.21ct.org/

■ **Association for the Advancement of
Computing in Education**
www.aace.org/

■ **Center for Media Literacy**
www.medialit.org/

■ **Choices Education Project**
www.brown.edu/Research/Choices/

■ **Cisco Educational Archive**
sunsite.unc.edu/cisco/cisco-home.html

■ **Crayola Art Education**
www.crayola.com/art_education/

■ **Developing Educational Standards**
putwest.boces.org/standards.html

■ **Education Week**
www.edweek.org/

■ **Educational Resources Information Center (ERIC)**
ericir.sunsite.syr.edu/

■ **Implicit Association Test**
depts.washington.edu/iat/

■ **InfoList for Teachers**
www.electriciti.com/rlakin/

■ **International WWW Schools Registry**
web66.coled.umn.edu/schools.html

■ **K-12+ Schools Web Site Index**
www.tenet.edu/education/main.html

■ **KinderArt**
www.kinderart.com/

■ **Learner Online**
www.learner.org/

■ **Multimedia Classrooms**
www.tcimet.net/mmclass/index.htm

■ **Natural Discovery Cave**
discovery.thorntons.co.uk/

■ **PBS TeacherSource**
www.pbs.org/teachersource/

■ **Rand Education**
info.rand.org/centers/iet/

■ **Scholastic Place**
www.scholastic.com/

■ **School Enrollment**
www.census.gov/population/www/
socdemo/school.html

■ **School.Net**
k12.school.net/

■ **Schoolroom Videos**
www.schoolroom.com/

■ **Story Arts**
www.storyarts.org/

■ **SyllabusWeb**
www.syllabus.com/

■ **Teacher Source**
www.pbs.org/teachersource/

■ **Teachers Helping Teachers**
www.pacificnet.net/~mandel/

■ **Teaching with Historic Places**
www.cr.nps.gov/nr/twhp/home.html

■ **Teachnet**
www.teachnet.com/

■ **The Thinking Fountain**
www.sci.mus.mn.us/sln/

■ **ThinkQuest**
www.thinkquest.org/

■ **U.S. Kids Compute**
www.uskidscompute.com/

■ **Xpeditions**
www.nationalgeographic.com/resources/
ngo/education/xpeditions/

Entertainment

The entertainment category is a big winner on the Internet, attracting everything from clowns to Elvis. See also Music, Sports, Movies, Games, *and* Television.

■ **Ain't It Cool News**
www.aint-it-cool-news.com/

■ **Arts and Entertainment**
www0.delphi.com/arts/

■ **As the Web Turns**
www.metzger.com/soap/cast.html

■ **Cirque de Soleil**
www.cirquedusoleil.com/

■ **Clown Hall of Fame**
www.webdom.com/chof/

- **Costume Source**
www.milieux.com/costume/source.html
- **Disney**
www.disney.com/
- **Electro Magnetic Poetry**
prominence.com/java/poetry/
- **Elvis Lives**
wsrv.clas.virginia.edu/~acs5d/elvis.html
- **Entertainment Charts**
www.worldcharts.nl/
- **Entertainment News**
www.muchmusic.com/rapidfax/
- **Faces**
www.corynet.com/faces/
- **Fireworks Central**
www.pcpros.net/~runrath/fireworks.html
- **Juggling**
www.juggling.org/
- **Klutz**
www.klutz.com/
- **Mr. Showbiz**
www.mrshowbiz.com/
- **Mungo Park**
www.mungopark.com
- **Second City**
www.secondcity.com/
- **Soundbites**
www.soundbites.com/

■ **The Station**
www.station.sony.com

■ **Ticketmaster**
www.ticketmaster.com

■ **Wizard of Oz**
www.thewizardofoz.com/

Entrepreneurs

The Internet is a natural for entrepreneurs who are starting on a shoestring. There are many experienced folks who offer information to help them along the way.

■ **20 Reasons**
www.net101.com/reasons.html

■ **Books and Software for the Entrepreneur**
www.business-plan.com/

■ **Bottom Up**
www.bottom-up.com/

■ **Business Know-How**
www.businessknowhow.com/

■ **Business Resource Center**
www.morebusiness.com/

■ **eCommerce Weekly**
www.eweekly.com/

■ **Entrepreneur America**
www.entrepreneur-america.org/

■ **Entrepreneur Book Store**
www.joem.com/

■ **Entrepreneur Magazine**
www.entrepreneurmag.com/magentre/
business_bytes.html

■ **Entrepreneurial Edge**
edgeonline.com/main/resourcepage/

■ **Entrepreneurial Parent**
www.en-parent.com/

■ **Entrepreneurs' Help Page**
www.tannedfeet.com/

■ **Entre-World**
www.entreworld.org/

■ **Global Entrepreneurs Network**
www.entrepreneurs.net/

■ **Great Idea Finder**
www.businessknowhow.com/

■ **Idea Café**
www.ideacafe.com/

■ **Minority Business Entrepreneur**
www.mbemag.com/

■ **Money Hunter**
www.moneyhunter.com/

■ **National Association for
the Self-Employed**
www.membership.com/nase/

■ **Score**
www.score.org/

■ **Small Business Internet Guide**
www.inlink.com/~turp182/html/
the_guide.html

■ **Virtual Entrepreneur**
www.virtualentrepreneur.com/

■ **WWW Entrepreneurial
Business Directory**
worldentre.com/bizdir.htm

Family

There are many resources on the Internet for families. See also Consumer Information *and* Kid Stuff.

■ **Adventure Bonding Parenting Page**
imageplaza.com/parenting/

■ **Ask Great-Granny**
www.mbnet.mb.ca/crm/granny/
granny.html

■ **Baby Names**
www.jellinek.com/baby/

■ **Baby Place**
www.baby-place.com/

■ **Babyonline**
www.babyonline.com/

■ **Baby-Proof Home**
www.babyproof.com/

■ **BlackFamilies**
www.blackfamilies.com/

■ **College Savings Plans**
www.collegesavings.org/

■ **Cybermom**
www.thecybermom.com/

■ **Facts for Families**
www.aacap.org/web/aacap/factsFam/

■ **Family EducationNetwork**
www.families.com/

■ **Family Internet**
www.familyinternet.com/

■ **Family Workshop**
www.ctw.org/

■ **Family.com**
www.family.go.com/

■ **Foster Parent Community**
www.fosterparents.com/

■ **Guide to Toys and Play**
www.kidsource.com/kidsource/content/
toys_ply.html

■ **Homearts**
www.homearts.com/

■ **Keeping Kids Reading**
www.tiac.net/users/maryl/

■ **Mommy Times**
www.mommytimes.com/

■ **Moms Online**
www.momsonline.com/

■ **Nap Time Notes**
www.ddc.com/napnotes/

■ **National Center for Fathering**
www.fathers.com/

■ **Parent Soup**
www.parentsoup.com/

■ **ParenthoodWeb**
www.parenthoodweb.com/

■ **Parenting Q & A**
www.parenting-qa.com/

■ **Parents at Home**
advicom.net/~jsm/moms/

■ **ParentsPlace**
www.parentsplace.com/

■ **Raisin**
www.raisinnet.com/

■ **Single and Custodial Father's Page**
www.single-fathers.org/

■ **Stork Net**
pages.prodigy.com/gifts/stork.htm

■ **Summer Camps**
www.camppage.com/

■ **WholeFamily Center**
www.wholefamily.com/

Festivals

These days, "festival" usually means "film festival."
But we were able to find a few of the traditional kind.

Festivals

■ **American Dance Festival**
www.americandancefestival.org/home.html

■ **Edinburgh Fringe Festival**
www.edfringe.com/

■ **Festival Finder**
www.festivalfinder.com/

■ **Festivals.com**
festivals.com/

■ **Festival Zone**
www.digitaal.com/festival/

■ **Lilith Fair**
www.lilithfair.com/

■ **National Asparagus Festival**
www.oceana.net/naf/

■ **New England Folk Festival**
www.ultranet.com/~neffa

■ **New Orleans Jazz and Heritage Festival**
www.nojazzfest.com/

■ **North Carolina Literary Festival**
sunsite.unc.edu/litfest/

■ **Oregon Shakespeare Festival**
www.orshakes.org/

■ **Prescott Park Arts Festival**
www.artfest.org/

■ **Rose of Tralee Festival**
homepages.iol.ie/~rose/

■ **What's Going On**
www.whatsgoingon.com/

Financial Aid

Here it is: most—if not all—the information available, all in one place.

■ **CollegeNET**
www.collegenet.com/

■ **Collegiate Funding Group**
www.collegiatefunding.com/

■ **Daedalus Company**
www.daedco.com/

■ **eStudentLoan**
www.estudentloan.com/

■ **fastWEB**
www.fastweb.com/fastweb/

■ **FinAid**
www.finaid.org/

■ **Financial Aid from U.S. Dept. of Education**
www.ed.gov/prog_info/SFA/StudentGuide/

■ **Financial Aid Resource Center**
www.theoldschool.org/

■ **Free Application for Federal Student Aid (FAFSA)**
www.fafsa.ed.gov/

■ **GoCollege**
www.gocollege.com

■ **Paying for College**
www.theoldschool.org/

■ **Private Funding Information**
www.rams.com/private.htm

■ **Resource Pathways**
www.collegeaid.com/

■ **Sallie Mae**
www.salliemae.com/

■ **Scholarship Resource Network**
www.rams.com/srn/

■ **Scholarship Search**
www.collegeboard.org/fundfinder/html/
ssrchtop.html

■ **Stafford Loans**
www.ed.gov/prog_info/SFA/StudentGuide/
1998-9/loan.html

■ **United Negro College Fund**
www.uncf.org/

Fitness and Health

If you are "into" fitness, you can find several use-
ful sites in this list. If you have avoided the
prospect, you might find some inspiration here.

■ **2nd Opinion**
www.2ndopinionstore.com/main.htm

■ **Achoo**
www.achoo.com

■ **American Medical Association**
www.ama-assn.org/

■ **Arthritis Foundation**
www.arthritis.org/

■ **Ask the Dietician**
www.dietitian.com/

■ **Black Stump Medical Page**
werple.net.au/~lions/medical.htm

■ **Cool Medical Site of the Week**
www.hooked.net/users/wcd/cmsotw.html

■ **Cool Running**
www.coolrunning.com/

■ **CyberDiet**
www.cyberdiet.com/

■ **Family Internet**
www.familyinternet.com/mhc/main.htm

■ **Fast Food Facts**
www.olen.com/food/

■ **Fitness Zone**
www.fitnesszone.com/

■ **Food Allergy Network**
www.foodallergy.org/

■ **Friends' Health Connection**
www.48friend.com/

■ **Go Ask Alice**
www.alice.columbia.edu/

■ **Go Get Fit**
www.lifetimetv.com/WoSport/gogetfit/

■ **Health Action Network Society**
www.hans.org/

■ **Health and Wellness Center**
shn.webmd.com/index.html

■ **Health Information Database**
chid.nih.gov/

■ **Health Mall**
www.hlthmall.com/

■ **Health-Center**
www.healthguide.com/

■ **Healthfinder**
www.healthfinder.gov

■ **HealthTouch**
www.healthtouch.com/

■ **HealthWorld Online**
www.healthy.net/

■ **Heart Preview Gallery**
sln2.fi.edu/biosci/preview/
heartpreview.html

■ **Heat Waves**
www.redcross.org/disaster/safety/heat.html

■ **HouseCall**
www.HouseCall.com/

■ **Internet Fitness Resource**
rampages.onramp.net/~chaz/

■ **Learn CPR**
www.learncpr.org/index.html

■ **Life Matters**
lifematters.com/

■ **Light Living**
www.lightliving.com/

■ **MD Interactive**
www.mit.edu/afs/athena/user/p/a/pandre/
www/

■ **Medical Breakthroughs**
www.ivanhoe.com/

■ **Medicine Box**
www.medicinebox.com/

■ **MedicineNet**
www.medicinenet.com/hp.asp?nc=Y

■ **Merck Manual**
www.merck.com/

■ **National Physique Committee**
www.getbig.com/info/npc.htm

■ **QuackWatch**
www.quackwatch.com/

■ **RxTV**
www.rxtv.com/

■ **Safe Within**
www.safewithin.com/

■ **SleepNet**
www.sleepnet.com/

■ **Thrive**
www.thriveonline.com/

■ **Video Fitness**
videofitness.com/

■ **Wellness Web**
www.wellweb.com/

■ **What Does It Take to Be Healthy?**
5aday.nci.nih.gov/

■ **Women's Health**
www.4women.gov/

■ **World Health Organization**
www.who.int/

■ **World Wellness on the Web**
wellness.uwsp.edu/

Food

Good but not necessarily good for you.

■ **Bagel Oasis**
www.bageloasis.com/

■ **Bread Recipe**
www.breadrecipe.com/

■ **Cakes**
www.cakerecipe.com/

■ **Chef Talk**
www.cheftalk.com/

■ **Chile-Heads**
neptune.netimages.com/~chile/

■ **CompuCook**
www.compucook.com/

■ **Cookie Recipes**
www.cookierecipe.com/

■ **Cooking Messy**
www.messygourmet.com/

▲ www.messygourmet.com

■ **Culinaria**
www.culinaria.com

■ **Digital Cookie**
www2.digitalcookie.com/cookie/

■ **Edible Insects**
www.eatbug.com/

■ **Epicurious**
www.epicurious.com/

■ **EthelM Chocolates**
www.ethelm.com

■ **Fast Food Facts**
www.olen.com/food/

■ **FlavorWeb**
www.flavorweb.com/

■ **Food and Drug Administration**
www.fda.gov/

■ **Food Network**
www.foodtv.com

■ **French Fries**
www.tx7.com/fries/

■ **Godiva Chocolates**
www.godiva.com/

■ **Gourmet World**
www.gourmetworld.com/

■ **Grits**
grits.com

■ **Gumbo Pages**
www.gumbopages.com/

■ **Homesick Gourmet**
homesickgourmet.radish.net/

■ **Inquisitive Cook**
www.inquisitivecook.com/

■ **International Food
Information Council**
ificinfo.health.org/

■ **Internet Chef**
www.ichef.com

■ **Jell-O**
www.kraftfoods.com/index.cgi?
brand=jell-o

■ **Kim-Chee**
www.kim-chee.com/

■ **Kitchen Link**
www.kitchenlink.com/

■ **Kosher Grocer**
www.koshergrocer.com/

■ **M&Ms Network**
www.m-ms.com/

■ **Meals for You**
www.mymenus.com/

■ **Meals**
www.meals.com

■ **Nantucket Nectars**
www.juiceguys.com/

■ **Planet Ketchup**
www.ketchup.wonderland.org/

■ **Popcorn Board**
www.popcorn.org/mpindex.htm

■ **Ragu Presents**
www.eat.com/

■ **Recipe Dude**
recipedude.com/

■ **RiceWeb**
www.riceweb.org/

■ **SmellTheCoffee**
www.smellthecoffee.com/

▲ www.smellthecoffee.com/

■ **Soup Recipes**
www.souprecipe.com/

■ **Star Chefs**
www.starchefs.com/

■ **Sushi Guide**
nmd.hyperisland.se/studentzone/crew2/
martin_ragnevad/

■ **Tastykake**
www.tastykake.com/

■ **Top Secret Recipes**
www.topsecretrecipes.com/

■ **Vegetarian Epicure**
www.vegetarianepicure.com/

Free Stuff

Entire books have been written about free stuff on the Internet. We were picky about what we selected.

■ **File Pile**
filepile.com/

■ **Free 'n Cool**
free-n-cool.com/

■ **Free and Neat Stuff**
www.abraxis.com/fans/

■ **Free Center**
www.freecenter.com/

■ **Free Site**
www.thefreesite.com/

■ Free Stuff Sites
www.thingamabob.com/

■ Free Stuff
www.tectonicdesigns.com/contest/
cindex.cgi?view=k

■ Jelly Belly
www.jellybelly.com/

■ Next to Nothing
www.winternet.com/~julie/ntn1.html

■ PC Computing Software Downloads
www.zdnet.com/pccomp/stories/all/
0,6605,383013,00.html

■ Post-It Notes
www.mmm.com/psnotes

■ Tool-Free Free Stuff
pages.prodigy.com/ULDE89A/

■ Volition Free Stuff Center
www.volition.com/free.html

Games and Puzzles

Some of these are multimedia sites.

■ Adenaline Vault
www.avault.com/

■ Backgammon on the Web
www.statslab.cam.ac.uk/~sret1/
backgammon/main.html

- **BaliHighway**
www.balihighway.com/

- **Bethesda Softworks**
www.bethsoft.com/

- **Big Top**
www.bigtop.com/

- **BigNetwork**
www.bignetwork.com/

- **Bingo Zone**
www.bingozone.com/

- **Buzzword Bingo**
www.buzzwordbingo.com/

- **Card Trick Central**
web.superb.net/cardtric

- **Checkers**
www.cs.caltech.edu/~vhuang/cs20/c/
applet/

- **Chess on the Net**
www.chessed.com/

- **Classic Board Games**
www.gamestorm.com/puzzleandboard/
classicboard/

- **Colony Wars**
www.colonywars.com/

- **Connect Four**
www.gamegate.com/connect4/

■ **Crossword Puzzle of the Day**
www.quizmaster.com/cotd.htm

■ **Cryptographs**
www.cryptograph.com/

■ **Dockingbay**
www.csd.uu.se/~johnn/

■ **DomainGames**
www.domaingames.com/

■ **Droodles**
www.webonly.com/droodles/index.html

■ **Electric Origami**
www.ibm.com/Stretch/EOS/

■ **Game Briefs**
www.gamebriefs.com/index.htm

■ **Game Guides**
www.gameguides.com/index.html

■ **Game Post**
www.gamepost.com/

■ **Game-Land**
www.game-land.com/

■ **Games Domain**
www.gamesdomain.co.uk/

■ **Gamesmania**
www.gamesmania.com/

■ **GameSpy**
www.gamespy.com/

■ **GT Interactive**
www.gtinteractive.com/

■ **Happy Puppy**
www.happypuppy.com

▲ www.happypuppy.com/

■ **Jeopardy**
www.station.sony.com/jeopardy/

■ **Mad Trivia**
www.madtrivia.com/

■ **Monopoly Probabilities**
www.teleport.com/~tcollins/
monopoly.shtml

■ **Monopoly**
www.monopoly.com/

■ **Mr. Edible Starchy Tuber Head**
winnie.acsu.buffalo.edu/potatoe/index.html

■ **Paintball Net**
www.paintball-net.com/

■ **Parcheesi**
www.rhodes.com/parcheesi/

■ **Phonetic**
www.phonetic.com

■ **Pooh Sticks**
pooh.muscat.co.uk/pooh-sticks/

■ **Puzzle Depot**
www.puzzledepot.com/

■ **Revenge of the Cow-Boy**
www.sega.com/multimedia/games/cow/

■ **Riddle du Jour**
www.dujour.com/riddle/

■ **Riddler**
www.riddler.com

■ **Rubik's Cube**
www.best.com/~schubart/rc/resources.html

■ **Scrabble**
www.scrabble.com/

■ **Stomped!**
www.stomped.com/

■ **Terra: Battle for the Outland**
www.kaon.com/

■ **Tiddlywinks**
www.tiddlywinks.org/

■ **Tic Tac Toe**
scv.bu.edu/Games/tictactoe

■ **Trivial Pursuit**
www.trivialpursuit.com/

■ Uproar
www.uproar.com

■ Weekend Edition Sunday Puzzle
www.npr.org/programs/wesun/puzzle.html

■ Wheel of Fortune
www.station.sony.com/wheel/

■ WordZap
www.wordzap.com/

■ You Don't Know Jack
www.won.net/gamerooms/bezerk/

Gardening

What's your pleasure? Terrariums? Giant pumpkins? Window boxes? Check it out.

■ Armchair Gardener
mailer.fsu.edu/~dansley/

■ Biological Control
www.nysaes.cornell.edu/ent/biocontrol/

■ Bloom
homearts.com/depts/garden/00gardc1.htm

■ Butterfly Gardens
www.uky.edu/Agriculture/Entomology/
entfacts/misc/ef006.htm

■ Cherry Blossom Gardens
www.garden-gifts.com/

■ City Farmer
www.cityfarmer.org/

■ **Daylilies**
www.daylilies.com/daylilies/

■ **Design Your Own Sprinkler System**
www.netyard.com/jsa/spklr.htm

■ **Dig**
www.digmagazine.com/

■ **Dirt Cheap Organics**
www.neteze.com/dB/index.htm

■ **Don't Panic Eat Organic**
www.rain.org/~sals/my.html

■ **Garden Escape**
www.garden.com/

■ **Garden Gate**
www.cityfarmer.org/

■ **Garden.com**
www.garden.com/

■ **Gardening in the South**
www.geocities.com/RainForest/Vines/8060

■ **GardenWeb**
www.gardenweb.com/

■ **Giant Pumpkins**
www.athenet.net/~dang/pumpkins.html

■ **Green Thumb**
www.hht.com/Bus/horns/green.htm

■ **Growing Vegetables at Home**
www.hoptechno.com/book26.htm

■ **Herb Gardening Charts**
www.ames.com/guides/herbs/charts.html

■ **Houseplant Care**
www.hoptechno.com/book26.htm

■ **Internet Shrine to the Tomato**
members.aol.com/rbi82/randy/
tomato.html#grow

■ **Interurban Water Farms**
www.interurban.com/

■ **Kootensaw Dovecotes**
www.dovecotes.co.uk/

■ **Landscaping to Attract Birds**
www.fws.gov/r9mbmo/pamphlet/
attract.html

■ **Lawn Care by State**
home.att.net/~dwis497002/states.htm

■ **Life in a Terrarium**
homearts.com/depts/garden/botanica/
01botab4.htm

■ **Master Composter**
www.mastercomposter.com/

■ **Proper Pruning**
aggie-horticulture.tamu.edu/extension/
pruning/pruning.html

■ **Rhododendron & Azaleas**
www.users.fast.net/~shenning/rhody.html

■ **Rooftop Gardens**
www.cityfarmer.org/rooftop59.html#rooftop

■ **Seeds Unique**
www.seedsonline.com/

■ **Spring Color**
www.springcolor.com/

■ **Traditional Gardening**
www.traditionalgardening.com/

■ **Understanding Your Soil**
homepages.which.net/~fred.moor/soil/
formed/f01.htm

■ **Urban Garden**
www.urbangarden.com/

■ **Virtual Garden**
www.vg.com/

■ **Weed Identification**
ext.agn.uiuc.edu/wssa/subpages/weed/
herbarium0.html

■ **Window Boxes**
www.sungro.com/conte-h.htm

■ **Yard-Care Answer Guy**
www.yardcare.com/

Genealogy

As a hobby, genealogy used to mean a lot of leg-work and letter writing. Now the Internet makes it so easy that genealogy has become a mainstream activity.

■ **Ancestry**
www.ancestry.com/

■ **Barrel of Genealogy Links**
cpcug.org/user/jlacombe/mark.html

■ **Carrie's Crazy Quilt**
www.mtjeff.com/~bodenst/page1.html

■ **Cool Sites for Genealogists**
www.cogensoc.org/cgs/cgs-cool.htm

■ **Cyndi's List of Genealogical Sites**
www.cyndislist.com/

■ **Everton's Genealogical Helper**
www.everton.com/

■ **Family Tree Maker Software**
www.familytreemaker.com

■ **Folks Online**
www.folksonline.com/bbs3/

■ **Genealogist's Index to the Web**
members.aol.com/genwebindx/index.htm

■ **Genealogy Abbreviations**
home.sprynet.com/~lgk71/2abbrevi.htm

■ **Genealogy Gateway**
www.polaris.net/~legend/listings/
listings.html

■ **Genealogy Home Page**
www.genhomepage.com/

■ **Genealogy Is My Hobby**
home.earthlink.net/~middleton/

■ **Genealogy Online**
www.genealogy.org/

■ **Genealogy Toolbox**
genealogy.tbox.com/

■ **Genealogy Unlimited**
www.itsnet.com/home/genun/public_html/

■ **Genealogy Web Search Tools**
www.gensource.com/

■ **How to Get Past the "Stone Wall"**
www.firstct.com/fv/stone.html

■ **International Black Sheep Society**
homepages.rootsweb.com/~blksheep/
index.html

■ **Italian Genealogy**
www.daddezio.com/

■ **Janyce's Root Diggin' Dept.**
www.janyce.com/gene/rootdig.html

■ **Journal of Online Genealogy**
www.onlinegenealogy.com/

■ **LDS Genealogy Records**
www.familysearch.org/

■ **Mayflower Web Page**
members.aol.com/calebj/mayflower.html

■ **National Genealogical Society**
www.genealogy.org/~ngs/

■ **Nova's Genealogy Page**
www.buffnet.net/~nova/

■ **RAND Genealogy Club**
info.rand.org/personal/Genea/

■ **Searchable Genealogy Links**
www.bc1.com/users/sgl/

■ **Surname Finder**
searches.rootsweb.com/

Government

The government was one of the earliest and biggest users of computers. It continued the pattern by being one of the earliest and biggest users of the Internet. Just about every government office and agency has a Web presence, and it is often easier to find information there than to contact an official—a real person—by telephone. We list only a few sites here; many others can be found under more specific titles.

■ **Congressional Information**
clerkweb.house.gov/

■ **Draft Registration Online**
www.sss.gov/

■ **FBI's Ten Most Wanted**
www.fbi.gov/toplist.htm

■ **Federal Web Locator**
www.law.vill.edu/Fed-Agency/fedwebloc.
html

■ **Internal Revenue Service**
www.irs.ustreas.gov

■ **Library of Congress**
www.loc.gov/

■ **Meet the Mayors**
www.mayors.org/

- **National Security Study Group**
www.nssg.gov/

- **Patent Web Databases**
www.uspto.gov/patft/

- **Social Security Online**
www.ssa.gov/SSA_Home.html

- **Terrorist Group Profiles**
web.nps.navy.mil/~library/tgp/tgpmain.htm

- **U.S. Census Bureau**
www.census.gov/

- **U.S. Patent and Trademark Office**
www.uspto.gov

- **U.S. Postal Service**
www.usps.gov/

- **U.S. Bill of Rights**
constitution.by.net/BillOfRights.html

- **U.S. Government Printing Office**
www.access.gpo.gov/index.html

- **U.S. Senate**
www.senate.gov

- **United States Government Manual**
www.access.gpo.gov/nara/browse-gm.html

- **White House**
www.whitehouse.gov/

Graphics—Animation

Those specifically interested in animation will find sites of interest in this list, but will probably be even more interested in the multimedia lists.

■ **3D Animated Flags**
www.3dflags.com/

■ **3D Café**
www.3dcafe.com/asp/default.asp

■ **3D Design Online**
www.3d-design.com/

■ **3D PixRay**
www.fortunecity.com/victorian/summit/
180/

■ **3Dize**
www.3dize.com/

■ **4U2C**
www.4u2c-us.com/4u2c.html

■ **A Touch of This**
www.atouchofthis.com/

■ **Alex's Animated Gif Shop**
www.wsdaents.com/

■ **Animated Banners**
www.mugs-n-more.com/main.htm

■ **Animated Gif Artist Guild**
www.agag.com/

■ **Animated Gifs**
www.angelfire.com/tx/willowrose/
animate.html

■ **Animated Holiday Gifs**
server2.powernet.net/~jograham/
holiday.htm

■ **Animation**
www.ogle.com/

■ **Animation and Graphics
for Your Web Site**
www.bellsnwhistles.com/

■ **Animation Express**
www.hotwired.com/animation/

■ **Animation Station**
www.animation-station.com/

■ **BoxTop Software**
www.boxtopsoft.com/

■ **Clip Flicks**
www.zurqui.com/crinfocus/clip/
flicks.html

■ **Computer Animation**
www.bergen.org/AAST/ComputerAnimation/

■ **Computer Graphics Lab**
ligsg2.epfl.ch/

■ **Destiny's Free Animated Gifs**
users.atnet.net/~mlosborn/

■ **Engineering Animation**
www.eai.com/index.html

■ **Facial Modeling and Animation**
www.cs.ubc.ca/nest/imager/contributions/
forsey/dragon/facial.html

■ **ForDyn Engineering Animation**
www.fordyn.com/

■ **Gallery of Animations**
members.tripod.com/adm/popup/
roadmap.shtml

■ **GFDL Visualization Guide Animation**
www.gfdl.gov/~jps/
GFDL_VG_Animation.html

■ **GifWorld**
www.gifworld.com/

■ **Gremlin Animation**
www.thegremlin.com/

■ **Hints for Web Animations**
www.cs.orst.edu/~pancake1/anim/

■ **HotWired Animation**
www.hotwired.com/animation/

■ **LightWork Design**
www.lightwork.com/

■ **Lotman's Animation Art Collection**
www.lotmansart.com/

■ **Lucasfilm**
www.lucasfilm.com/

■ **Millanimations**
www.millan.net/anims/giffar.html

■ **Misery Graphics**
www.itprojects.net/~den/

■ **MPEG Embedded Animation**
www.cs.orst.edu/~pancake1/anim/test/
blur_mpeg_embedded.html

■ **PepWorks**
www2.pepworks.com/pepworks/

■ **S/R Lab Animation**
www.srlabs.com/

■ **UCLA Animation Workshop**
animation.filmtv.ucla.edu/

■ **Women in Animation**
women.in.animation.org/

Graphics—Fractals

Fractal art is formed by using the computer to repeat geometric shapes with color, size, and angle variations.

■ **Crazy Fractals**
ourworld.compuserve.com/homepages/
pete_and_glyn/

■ **Fantastic Fractals**
library.advanced.org/12740/cgi-bin/login.cgi

■ **Fractal Desktop**
fractaldesktop.virtualave.net/

■ **Fractal Division**
members.tripod.com/~Jayell/Gallery.html

■ **Fractal Domains**
www.fractaldomains.com/

■ **Fractal Images**
www.softsource.com/fractal.html

■ **Fractal Images**
www.maui.com/~twright/fractals/
fractals.html

■ **Fractal Journey of the Season**
www.cybercom.net/~kmcguire/fractal.htm

■ **Fractal Microscope**
www.ncsa.uiuc.edu/Edu/Fractal/
Fractal_Home.html

■ **Fractal Pictures and Animations**
www.cnam.fr/fractals.html

■ **Fractal World**
www.kcsd.k12.pa.us/~projects/fractal/

■ **Fractals Lesson**
math.rice.edu/~lanius/frac/

■ **Sekino's Fractal Gallery**
www.willamette.edu/~sekino/fractal/
fractal.htm

■ **Sprott's Fractal Gallery**
sprott.physics.wisc.edu/fractals.htm

■ **The Fractory**
tqd.advanced.org/3288/

■ **Ultra Fractal**
ourworld.compuserve.com/homepages/
slijkerman/screen.htm

■ **What Are Fractals?**
www.fractals.com/tfic/html/fractals.html

Graphics—Free Stuff for Your Home Page

Many sites have made their icons and images freely available. You can copy what you want for use on your own home page.

■ **...connected**
www.connected-media.com/

■ **A+ Clip Art**
aplusart.simplenet.com/aplusart/index.html

■ **Absolutely Free Icon Library**
www.free-search.com/afil/

■ **Angelfire**
www.angelfire.com/

■ **Background Color Switcher**
www.urban75.com/Mag/java3.html

■ **Background Colors**
www.halcyon.com/godlbaum/backclrs.htm

■ **Background Sampler**
www.netscape.com/assist/net_sites/bg/
backgrounds.html

■ **Banner Generator**
www.coder.com/creations/banner/

■ **Barry's Clip Art**
www.barrysclipart.com/

■ **Borders by Silverhair**
www.toolcity.net/~tshaw/main.htm

■ **Buttons, Bullets, and Backgrounds**
www.rewnet.com/bbb/

■ **Caboodles Clip Art**
www.caboodles.com

■ **Cartoon Animals**
www.toontakes.com/WebArt.html

■ **Clip Art Connection**
www.clipartconnection.com/

■ **Clip Art Searcher**
www.webplaces.com/search/

■ **Clip Art Universe**
www.nzwwa.com/mirror/clipart/

■ **Clipart Castle**
www.clipartcastle.com/

■ **Clipart.com**
www.clipart.com/

■ **CoolText**
www.cooltext.com/

■ **Customized License Plate**
www.dewa.com/plate/main-99.shtml

■ **Elated Web Toolbox**
www.elated.com/toolbox/

■ **Free Image Repository**
www.planetnetwork.com/exp4/index.htm

■ **Graphics Depot**
www.graphicsdepot.com/

■ **Humble Bee**
www.isholf.is/DESEMBER/

■ **Iconographics Design**
www.iconographics.com/clip_f.htm

■ **Image O Rama**
members.aol.com/dcreelma/imagesite/
image.htm

■ **Images and Icons**
www.stars.com/Vlib/Authoring/
Images_and_Icons.html

■ **Inki's ClipArt**
www.inki.com/clipart/

■ **Interactive Features**
interactivefeatures.com/

■ **Internet Bumper Stickers**
www.directtodave.com/ibs/

■ **Kita Lab Icon Archive**
www-a2k.is.tokushima-u.ac.jp/member/kita/
cgi-bin/icon.cgi

■ **Little Wing Gallery**
www.hal-pc.org/~dunmar/littlewing/gallery/
galryind.html

■ **Logo Design**
www.coolgraphic.com/

■ **Over the Rainbow**
www.geocities.com/SiliconValley/Heights/
1272/rainbow.html

■ **Pardon My Icons**
www.zeldman.com/icon.html

■ **Pattern Land**
www.netcreations.com/patternland/

■ **Rad Graphics**
www.rad-gfx.com/

■ **Signboard**
www.tiac.net/users/tobey/signboard/

■ **Silk Purse Graphics**
mars.ark.com/~rhamstra/backgrnd.html

■ **Texture Land**
www.meat.com/textures/

■ **Texture Station**
www.nepthys.com/textures/

■ **Tweety Pie's Clip Art Collection**
www.ltexpress.com/ndxbox1.html

Graphics—General

Graphics are one of the major bonuses of computing. Pictures are a vast improvement over plain text.

■ **3D Café**
www.3dcafe.com/

■ **3D Ring**
3d-spotlite.3dark.com/3d-ring/

■ **3m Image Graphics**
www.mmm.com/imagegraphics/

■ **ACM SIGGRAPH**
www.siggraph.org/home.html

■ **Bozlo Beaver**
www.bozlo.com/

■ **Computer Graphics Links**
mambo.ucsc.edu/psl/cg.html

■ **Cool Demos**
www-graphics.stanford.edu/demos/

■ **Corbis**
www.corbis.com/

■ **EyeWire**
www.imageclub.com/

■ **Free Graphics for Your Web Page**
mem.tcon.net/users/5010/6293/index.htm

■ **Grafica Obscura**
www.sgi.com/grafica/

■ **Graphic Home**
www.graphic-home.iok.net/

■ **Graphic Linx**
www.graphiclinx.com/

■ **Graphics Links**
www.hitline.ch/ger/homepage/jacob/
gratis.htm

■ **Graphics User**
www.zdnet.com/products/graphicsuser/
index.html

■ **Hey You! Graphics**
hey-you.com/collective/

■ **Image of the Day**
www.metatools.com/galleries/iotd/

■ **Image Surfer**
isurf.interpix.com/

■ **Internet Ray Tracing Competition**
www.irtc.org

■ **Introduction to Imaging**
www.ahip.getty.edu/intro_imaging/

■ **Lightscape**
www.lightscape.com/

■ **Macintosh Graphics Resources**
www.users.interport.net/%7Ejashear/
mac_graphics.html

■ **Marc Yankus**
www.users.interport.net/~niceboy/portfolio/

■ **Matrox Group**
www.matrox.com/

■ **Pamorama**
www.pamorama.com/

■ **Phong**
www.phong.com/

■ **Pixel Foundary**
www.pixelfoundry.com/

■ **Pixelplace**
www.pixelplace.com/

■ **Pixelsight**
www.pixelsight.com/

■ **Raytracing FAQs**
www.povray.org/documents/rayfaq/
rayfaq.html

- **Realm Graphics**
www.ender-design.com/rg/
- **Stanford Computer Graphics**
www-graphics.stanford.edu
- **TheISpot**
www.theispot.com/
- **Transparent Background Images**
members.aol.com/htmlguru/
transparent_images.html
- **Vision Quest**
www.boondock.com/visionquest/
- **Volumeone**
www.volumeone.com
- **Webpedia Graphics**
www.webpedia.com/cooltype/?

Graphics—Screen Savers

Most, but not all, of these screen savers can be downloaded free.

- **Ansel Adams Screensavers**
www.digitalwow.com/screenlogic/ansel.htm
- **ArtScreens**
www.artscreens.com/
- **Cities Screensaver**
www.design2graphics.com/html/ssaver/
ssaver_cities.html

- **Great Smoky Mountains Screensaver**
www.greatsmokymtns.com/

- **Holographic Screen Saver**
www.virtual-creations.com/

- **Jumbo Screen Savers**
www.jumbo.com/pages/mm/ss/

- **Kaleidoscope**
www.syntrillium.com/kaleidoscope/index.html

- **Lilli's Free Screen Savers**
www.lilli.clara.net/freesaver/

- **Make Your Own Screen Saver**
www.customsavers.com/

- **Psychedelic Screen Saver**
www.synthesoft.com/psych/psych.htm

- **Screen Saver Heaven**
www.galttech.com/ssheaven.shtml

- **Screen Savers Bonanza**
www.bonanzas.com/ssavers/

- **ScreenSaver**
www.screensaver.com/

- **Screentheme**
www.screenthemes.com/

Graphics—Software

Some are expensive professional products, some shareware. Several have galleries.

■ **Adobe Photoshop Web Reference**
www.adscape.com/eyedesign/photoshop/

■ **Adobe**
www.adobe.com/

■ **Autocad Shareware Clearinghouse**
www.cadalog.com/

■ **Bryce Tips and Tricks**
www.kagi.com/busse/BSolutions/
BSolutions.html

■ **Bryce Tutorials**
www.ruku.com/bryce.html

■ **CorelDraw**
www.corel.com/

■ **Imagine Graphics**
www.imaginegraphics.org/

■ **Lightwave 3D**
www.newtek.com/

■ **Marlin Studios Graphics Machine**
www.stmuc.com/moray/

■ **Moray Home Page**
www.stmuc.com/moray/

■ **Paint Shop Pro Tips**
psptips.com/

■ **Photoshop Tips**
www.mccannas.com/pshop/photosh0.htm

■ **POV-Ray**
www.povray.org/

■ **Ray Dream Studio**
www.raydream.com/products/rds/

■ **Rhino**
www.rhino3d.com/

■ **Terrain Maker**
www.ericjorgensen.com/html/tm.htm

History

Both organizations and academic institutions have made use of the Internet to tell the story of the world, one chunk at a time.

■ **1939 World's Fair**
xroads.virginia.edu/~1930s/DISPLAY/39wf/front.htm

■ **1968: The Whole World Was Watching**
www.stg.brown.edu/projects/1968/

■ **Abridged History of the United States**
www.us-history.com/

■ **Academy of Achievement**
www.achievement.org/autodoc/pagegen/mainmenu.html?hb=1

■ **American Civil War**
sunsite.utk.edu/civil-war/

■ **American Memory**
rs6.loc.gov

■ **American West**
www.AmericanWest.com/

■ **Ancient World Web**
www.julen.net/aw/

■ **Battle of Hastings 1066**
battle1066.com/

■ **Benjamin Franklin**
sln.fi.edu/franklin/rotten.html

■ **Betsy Ross**
libertynet.org/iha/betsy/index.html

■ **Black History Tour**
library.advanced.org/10320/Tourmenu.htm

■ **British Monarchy**
www.royal.gov.uk/

■ **California Gold Rush**
www.sjmercury.com/goldrush/
goldrush_resources.shtml

■ **Civil War: An Illinois Soldier**
www.ioweb.com/civilwar/

■ **Child Labor in America**
www.historyplace.com/unitedstates/
childlabor/index.html

■ **Colonial Williamsburg**
www.history.org/

■ **Ellis Island**
www.ellisisland.org/

■ **French and Indian War**
web.syr.edu/~laroux/

■ **Gateway to World History**
www.hartford-hwp.com/gateway/

■ **Great Chicago Fire**
www.chicagohs.org/fire/

■ **Guts and Glory**
www.pbs.org/wgbh/pages/amex/guts/

■ **Harappa**
www.harappa.com/

■ **Harlem Renaissance**
harlem.eb.com/

■ **Historical U.S. Census Data**
fisher.lib.virginia.edu/census/

■ **History Buff**
www.historybuff.com/

■ **History Net**
www.thehistorynet.com/

■ **History of Money**
www.ex.ac.uk/~RDavies/arian/llyfr.html

■ **Horus' History Links**
www.ucr.edu/h-gig/horuslinks.html

■ **HyperHistory**
www.hyperhistory.com/

■ **Journey on the Underground Railroad**
www.smithsonianmag.si.edu/smithsonian/issues96/oct96/undergroundrr.html

■ **Kennedy Tapes**
www.cs.umb.edu/jfklibrary/tapes_1998.html

■ **Lewis and Clark**
www.pbs.org/lewisandclark/

■ **Martin Luther King Papers**
www.stanford.edu/group/King/

■ **Monticello**
www.monticello.org/

■ **Organization of American Historians**
www.indiana.edu/~oah/

■ **Panama Canal**
www.discovery.com/stories/history/panama/
panama.html

■ **People's Century**
www.pbs.org/wgbh/peoplescentury/

■ **Pop History Now**
www.bestpractices.org/

■ **Rulers**
www.geocities.com/Athens/1058/
rulers.html

■ **Seven Wonders**
pharos.bu.edu/Egypt/Wonders/

■ **Somme Battle 1916**
www.btinternet.com/~sommetours/

■ **This Day in History**
www.historychannel.com/today/

■ **U-boat Net**
uboat.net/

■ **Vietnam Veteran's Wall**
www.thevirtualwall.org/

■ **Women in American History**
women.eb.com/

■ **World History Document Archives**
www.hartford-hwp.com/archives/

Hobbies and Interests

Have we mentioned your hobby in this list? Possibly not. We tried to present a representative sample. See also Gardening, Cycling, Outdoor Recreation, *and* Sports.

■ **AeroWeb**
aeroweb.brooklyn.cuny.edu/

■ **American Kiteflyers Association**
www.aka.kite.org/

■ **Antique Radios**
members.aol.com/djadamson/arp.html

■ **AquaLink**
www.aqualink.com/

■ **Autograph Central**
www.concentric.net/~nykk/autograf.htm

■ **Beekeeping**
ourworld.compuserve.com/homepages/
Beekeeping/

■ **Card Collector Link**
www.collector-link.com/cards/

■ **Center for Puppetry Arts**
www.puppet.org/

■ **Chinook Checkers**
www.cs.ualberta.ca/~chinook/

■ **Classic Typewriters**
xavier.xu.edu/~polt/typewriters.html

■ **Coin Universe**
www.coin-universe.com/

■ **Collecting Cuff Links**
www.cufflink.com/

■ **CraftNet Village**
www.craftnet.org/

■ **Crafts Galore**
www.massachusetts.net/nozzle/crafts/

■ **Disneyananet**
www.disneyananet.com/

■ **Gold Prospecting**
www.klws.com/gold/gold.html

■ **Handwriting**
www.hy.com/

■ **Historical Bottle Collectors**
www.av.qnet.com/~glassman/

■ **Hobby Stores on the Net**
www.hobbystores.com/

■ **HobbyWorld**
www.hobbyworld.com/

■ **International Paperweight Society**
www.armory.com/~larry/ips.html

■ **Internet Antique Shop**
www.tias.com/

■ **Juggling**
www.juggling.org/

■ **Knappers Anonymous**
www.ucs.mun.ca/~t64tr/knap.html

■ **Knots on the Web**
www.earlham.edu/~peters/knotlink.htm

■ **License Plates of the World**
danshiki.oit.gatech.edu/~iadt3mk/
index.html

■ **Magic Theater**
magictheater.com/index.html

■ **MagicTricks**
www.magictricks.com/

■ **Origami Flowers**
www.the-village.com/origami/gallery.html

■ **Paper Folding**
www.sgi.com/grafica/fold/page001.html

■ **Pez Memorabilia**
www.spectrumnet.com/pez/

■ **Puzzle Depot**
www.puzzledepot.com/

■ **Quilting Page**
ttsw.com/MainQuiltingPage.html

■ **Rockhounds Information Page**
www.rahul.net/infodyn/rockhounds/
rockhounds.html

■ **Scrolling Mystery Theatre**
www.fiction.com/

■ **Shortwave Radio**
itre.ncsu.edu/radio/

■ **Society for Creative Anachronism**
www.sca.org/

■ **Speleology**
hum.amu.edu.pl/~sgp/spec/links.html

■ **Stamp Shows**
www.stampshows.com/

■ **Trendy Magic**
trendy.org/magic/interactivemagic.html

■ **Tried & True Trains**
www.tttrains.com/

■ **U.S. Mint Stamps**
www.best.com/~mleon/usmints.html

■ **Vexillology**
www.midcoast.com/~martucci/Vex.html

■ **Virtual Flyshop**
www.flyshop.com/

■ **World Collectors Net**
www.worldcollectorsnet.com/

Home Page Advice

Folks on the Internet are anxious to tell you how to write your own home page on the Web.

■ **Auditorial.com**
www.auditorial.com/

■ **Avoiding Dithering Colors**
www.sirius.com/~industry/consider.html

■ **BigNoseBird**
bignosebird.com/

▲ bignosebird.com/

■ **Browser-safe Color Palette**
www.lynda.com/hex.html

■ **Color on the Web**
www.adobe.com/newsfeatures/palette/
main.html

■ **Creating a Successful Web Page**
www.hooked.net/~larrylin/web.htm

■ **Creating Killer Websites**
www.killersites.com/

■ **EarthWeb Tutorials**
www.developer.com/classroom/tutorials/

■ **Elements of Web Design**
builder.cnet.com/Graphics/Design/

■ **Framing the Web**
webreference.com/dev/frames/

■ **Glassdog's Design-O-Rama**
www.glassdog.com/design-o-rama/
webdesign.html

■ **Hands-on Training by DocOzone**
www.visi.com/~drozone/handson/

■ **Homepager's Web Site Resources**
www.homepagers.com/resour/htm1.html

■ **Idiot's Guide to Making a Home Page**
www.voyager.co.nz/~bsimpson/html.htm

■ **I-Doctor**
abirc.com/help.htm

■ **Internet Bag Lady**
www.dumpsterdive.com/

■ **iSyndicate**
www.isyndicate.com/

■ **Learn Web Publishing**
www.learnthenet.com/english/section/
webpubl.html

■ **Make Some Noise**
builder.cnet.com/Authoring/Audio/

■ **Modular Graphics**
www.zurqui.com/crinfocus/mod/leggo.html

■ **Net Ezy**
www.netezy.com/resources.htm

■ **Net Tips for Writers and Designers**
www.dsiegel.com/tips/index.html

■ **NetGuru**
www.netguru.com/

■ **Peoplesphere**
www.peoplesphere.com/

■ **Project Cool**
projectcool.com/

■ **SpiderSchool**
www.artswire.org/Artswire/spiderschool/
spider.htm

■ **ReallyBig**
reallybig.com/default.shtml

■ **Sun Guide to Web Style**
www.sun.com/styleguide/

■ **Ten Top Mistakes**
www.useit.com/alertbox/9706b.html

■ **Tips and Tricks**
www5.metacreations.com/community/tips/
index.html

■ **TipWorld**
www.tipworld.com/

■ **Web Authoring FAQ**
www.htmlhelp.com/faq/html/all.html

■ **Web Design Tips**
www.colin.mackenzie.org/webdesign/

■ **Web Development Resources**
www.eborcom.com/webmaker/

■ **Web Page Design**
ds.dial.pipex.com/pixelp/wpdesign/
wpdintro.htm

■ **Web Site Garage**
www.websitegarage.com/

- **■ Web Weenie**
w3.i-us.com/

- **■ WebHome Improvement**
www.htmltips.com/

- **■ Webspawner**
www.webspawner.com/

- **■ WebSter's Dictionary**
www.goldendome.net/Tools/WebSter/

- **■ Yale Web Style Guide**
info.med.yale.edu/caim/manual/

Home Page—Free Space

These folks, for the most part, offer free disk space and Web hosting services for your home page. Some offer technical advice and some even make the page for you. Be aware also that most sites limit page content, prohibiting, for example, advertising or adult material.

- **■ 1-2-Free My Page**
www.1-2-free.com/mypage

- **■ Acme City**
www.acmecity.com/

- **■ Aid 4**
www.y4i.com/freeusa.html

- **■ Angelfire**
www.angelfire.com/index.shtml

- **■ B-City**
www.bcity.com/bcity/

■ **BraveNet**
www.bravenet.com/
free_webtools_for_webmasters.htm

▲ www.bravenet.com/
free_webtools_for_webmasters.htm

■ **Compu-Pro**
gocompupro.com/users/index.shtml

■ **Crosswinds**
www.crosswinds.net/

■ **Cybercities**
www.cybercities.com/

■ **Cyberplace**
cyberplace.hypermart.net/index.htm

■ **Fiberia Free Web Pages**
home.fiberia.com/root/bottom.html

■ **Free Web Space Providers Guide**
www.mediaport.org/~freepage/fpage1.htm

■ **Free Webspace.Net**
www.freewebspace.net/

■ **FreeTown**
www.freetown.com/free/index.html

■ **FreeYellow**
www.freeyellow.com/

■ **GeoCities**
www.geocities.com

■ **Homestead**
www.homestead.com/

■ **HowdyNeighbor**
www.howdyneighbor.com/

■ **Net Guide Free Web Hosting**
www.netguide.com/Snapshot/
Archive?guide=internet&id=831

■ **Nettaxi Online Communities**
www.nettaxi.com/

■ **OneStop Network**
www.onestop.net/

■ **Ostriches Online**
www.achiever.com/design/freehmpg.html

■ **Personal Web Pages**
home.att.net/index.html

■ **Space Ports**
www.spaceports.com/

■ **Theglobe.com**
www.theglobe.com/

■ **Towne Square**
townsquare.usr.com/

■ **Tripod**
www.tripod.com/build/

■ **Website Publishing and Hosting**
www.byop.com/

■ **XOOM**
xoom.com/home/

Home Page—HTML Help Sites

Each of these sites offers information in its own way. Find the ones most helpful to you.

■ **Ask Dr. Web**
www.zeldman.com/faq.html

■ **Bare Bones HTML**
werbach.com/barebones/

■ **Beginner's Guide to HTML**
www.web-nation.com/lessons/html-pri.htm

■ **Beginner's Guide to HTML**
www.ncsa.uiuc.edu/General/Internet/WWW
/HTMLPrimer.html

■ **Beyond the Bones of HTML**
www.avalon.net/~librarian/bones/

■ **Composing Good HTML**
www.cs.cmu.edu/~tilt/cgh/

■ **Dark Side of HTML**
www.best.com/~sem/dark_side/

■ **Elements of HTML Style**
www.book.uci.edu/Staff/StyleGuide.html

■ **How Do They Do That with HTML?**
www.nashville.net/~carl/htmlguide/

■ **HTML Bad Style**
www.earth.com/bad-style/

■ **HTML Goodies**
www.htmlgoodies.com/

■ **HTML Guide**
www.emerson.emory.edu/services/html/
html.html

■ **HTML Quick Reference**
web.canlink.com/webdesign/htmlcard.html

■ **Interactive HTML Tutorial
for Beginners**
davesite.com/webstation/html/

■ **Introduction to HTML**
www.cwru.edu/help/introHTML/toc.html

■ **Meta-Tag Generator**
www.websitepromote.com/resources/meta/

■ **NetMechanic**
www.netmechanic.com/

Home Page Publicity

If tinkering with your home page is a favorite pastime, then check out these sites, all devoted to helping you publicize your home page. Some sites offer free service; others charge a fee. Some also explain how to hone your page so that it will be picked up by search engines.

■ 101 Promotion Service
www.kwik-link.com/c/promote.htm

■ AddURL
submitit.linkexchange.com/

■ Central Registry
www.centralregistry.com/

■ Global Links
www.vicom.net/global/

■ Hit Man
www.webthemes.com/hitman.html

■ Internet Promotions Megalist
www.centralregistry.com/

■ Launch-it
www.launch-it.com/

■ Multi-Submit
users.boone.net/yinon/multisub/
default.html

■ NetPost
www.netpost.com/netpost2.html

■ PostMaster
www.netcreations.com/postmaster/

■ Register It
www.register-it.com/

■ **Site Promoter**
www.sitepromoter.com/

■ **Submit Blaster**
www.ansur.net/

■ **Submit It!**
www.submit-it.com/

■ **Submit to Search Engines
and Directories**
www.aniota.com/~jwhite/submit.html

■ **Virtual Promote**
www.virtualpromote.com/

■ **Website Promoter Center**
www.wprc.com/

■ **WebStep Top 100**
www.mmgco.com/top100.html

Houses—Buying and Selling

Buying, building, selling. See also Architecture.

■ **4 Sale by Owner**
www.byownersales.com/

■ **All About Home**
www.allabouthome.com/

■ **American Builders Network**
americanbuilders.com/

■ **Ask the Builder**
www.askbuild.com/

■ **Buy-a-Farm**
www.buy-a-farm.com/

▲ www.buy-a-farm.com/

■ **By Owner Online**
www.by-owner-ol.com/

■ **E-Loan**
www.eloan.com/

■ **Glossary of Real Estate and Mortgage Terms**
www.vamch.com/reinfo.html

■ **Holiday Junction**
www.holidayjunction.com/

■ **Home Inspection SuperSite**
www.inspectamerica.com/index.htm

■ **Home Starter Kit**
www.homepath.com/hsp1.html

■ **Homefair**
americanbuilders.com/

■ **HomeNet**
www.netprop.com/

■ **Homeowners Finance Center**
www.homeowners.com/

■ **HomePath**
www.homepath.com/

■ **International Real Estate Digest**
www.ired.com/

■ **Internet Design Center**
www.internetdesigncenter.com/

■ **Internet Realty Network**
www.gorealty.com/contents.html

■ **ListingLink**
listinglink.com/

■ **Mover Quotes**
moverquotes.com/

■ **NewHomeSearch**
www.newhomesearch.com/

■ **Open House America**
www.openhouse.net/

■ **Property America**
www.propertyamerica.com/

■ **Quicken Mortgage**
www.quickenmortgage.com/

■ **Realtor.com**
www.realtor.com/

■ **Realty Advisor**
www.realtyadvisor.com/

■ **Realty Locator**
www.realtylocator.com/

■ **Relocate America**
www.nationwidehomes.com/

■ **Relocation Central**
www.relocationcentral.com/

■ **Rural Estate Network**
www.ruralspace.com/

■ **The Home Buying Process**
www.interest.com/mortimer.html

■ **Virtual Relocation**
www.virtualrelocation.com/

Houses—Remodeling and Repairing

Need some help with repairs around the house?
All kinds of folks are ready to offer assistance.

■ **BH&G Home Improvement Encyclopedia**
www.bhglive.com/homeimp/

■ **Building and Remodeling Resources**
www.buildandremodel.com/

■ **Energy Outlet**
www.energyoutlet.com/

■ **Fix-It**
begin.com/fixit/

■ **HearthNet**
hearth.com/

■ **Home Ideas**
www.homeideas.com/

■ **Home Improvement and Repair**
www.hometime.com/

■ **Home Improvement Highway**
www.csz.com/hih/

■ **Home Improvement Tips**
www.housenet.com/

■ **Home Lighting**
www.homelighting.com/

■ **Homebuyer's Fair**
www.homefair.com/home/

■ **Household Cyclopedia**
members.xoom.com/mspong/

■ **HouseNet**
www.housenet.com/

■ **ImproveNet**
www.improvenet.com/

▲ www.improvenet.com/

■ **Kitchen-Bath**
www.kitchen-bath.com/

■ **LivingHome**
www.livinghome.com/

■ **Owners' Network**
www.owners.com/

■ **Paint Estimator**
www.bhglive.com/homeimp/docs/
v0000041.htm

■ **Pete's Dry Dock**
www.buildingwithbob.com/

■ **Remodeling Online**
www.remodeling.hw.net/

■ **Today's Homeowner**
www.todayshomeowner.com/repair/index.
html

■ **Toolsource**
www.remodeling.hw.net/

■ **True Value**
www.truevalue.com/index.asp

How To . . .

There are many sites that offer comprehensive advice or instructions. Not here. These sites offer limited information on a limited topic, some serious and some frivolous. The titles here reflect what they offer.

■ **Adopt a Wolf**
www.teleport.com/~wnorton/wolfadop.
html

■ **Apply for U.S. citizenship**
home.earthlink.net/~bobodonnell/apply.
html

■ **Be better off a year from now**
www.ymcpa.com/article2.htm

■ **Breakdance**
www.howtobreakdance.com/

■ **Build a frame loom**
www.hallnet.com/build.html

■ **Carve a jack-o-lantern**
www.jack-o-
lantern.com/patterns/patterns.html

■ **Cite Internet sources in research papers**
www.cgrg.ohio-state.edu/interface/W96/
page.html

■ **Claim your unclaimed money**
www.foundmoney.com/

■ **Create a child genius**
www.hkmlog.com/ChildGenus.html

■ **Do CPR**
www.amherst.edu/~jaloduca/cpr.html

■ **Do tombstone rubbings**
www.firstct.com/fv/t_stn1.html

■ **Drive a railway locomotive**
www.geocities.com/ad_container/
pop.html?cuid=10203&keywords=none

■ **Escape from a boring job**
www.quick.net/lfc/seekers/escape.html

■ **Find a lost friend**
www.lost-and-found.com/lfc/locate.html

■ **Form a cooperative**
www.mncoop.org/how-step3.htm

■ **Get a passport**
travel.state.gov/index-howto.html

■ **Get Russian fonts**
www.city.ru/rusfonts.htm

■ Get the exact time
tycho.usno.navy.mil

■ Get your way at the auto dealer
www.edmunds.com/edweb/usedinfo/
contents.html

■ Guide the blind
biomed.nus.sg/access/guideblind.html

■ Juggle
www.jestdandy.com/howtojuggle.htm

**■ Keep your blood pressure
under control**
www.coolware.com/health/
medical_reporter/hypertension.html

■ Learn a new fact each day
www.cool-fact.com/today/

■ Make a kite
www.interlog.com/~excells/kites/make.html

■ Make a pie crust
www.teleport.com/~psyched/pie/crust.html

■ Make a pop-up card
www.makersgallery.com/joanirvine/
howto.html

■ Make a violin
www.graffiti.it/stradivari/photostory/
storybrd.html

■ Make Vietnamese noodle soup
www.best.com/~phohoa

■ Play Go
www.webwind.com/go/goLes/goLes1.htm

■ **Prepare for an earthquake**
quake.usgs.gov/

■ **Prevent the spread of weeds**
www.blm.gov/education/weeds/weed.html

■ **Protect yourself from auto theft**
www.watchyourcar.org/index2.html

■ **Remove a stain**
www.clothesline.com/stainDet/index.html

■ **Start a business**
www.inreach.com/sbdc/book/toc.html

■ **Unclog a drain**
www.clickit.com/bizwiz/homepage/
plumber.htm

■ **Use fresh culinary herbs**
www.herbthyme.com/howtous.htm

■ **Write a complaint letter**
www-csag.cs.uiuc.edu/individual/pakin/
complaint

Humor

Much humor on the Internet is funny indeed, but a lot of it is simply terrible. We tried to present an inoffensive sampling.

■ **Argon Zark**
www.zark.com/front/hub.html

■ **Art Faux Fine Art Gallery**
www.pcmagic.net/cpinckney/

■ **Bob's Fridge Door**
www.bobsfridge.com/

■ **Calvin and Hobbes**
www.uexpress.com/ups/comics/ch/

■ **Cartoon Network**
www.cartoonnetwork.com/wpt/index.html

■ **Cartoon World**
www.cet.com/~rascal/

■ **Cathy**
www.uexpress.com/ups/comics/ca/

■ **Centre for the Easily Amused**
www.amused.com/

■ **Chickenhead**
www.chickenhead.com/

■ **Comedy Central**
www.comcentral.com

■ **Common Boundaries**
www.commonb.com/comics/

■ **Crimson Empire**
www.starwars.com/crimson/index.html

■ **Daily Muse**
www.cais.com/aschnedr/muse.htm

■ **DC Comics**
www.dccomics.com/

■ **Dilbert Zone**
www.dilbert.com/

■ **Doonesbury**
www.doonesbury.com/

■ **Funny**
www.funny.co.uk/

■ **FunTrivia**
funtrivia.com/

■ **Gibbleguts**
www.gibbleguts.com/frameset2.htm

■ **Ha!**
www.hardyharhar.com/

■ **Humor Search**
www.humorsearch.com/

■ **I Hate Computers**
extlab1.entnem.ufl.edu/IH8PCs/index.html

■ **Internet Funny Pages**
www.its.bldrdoc.gov/%7Ebing/cartoons.
html

■ **Internet Squeegee Guy**
www.website1.com/squeegee/

■ **Manic Media**
www.epgmedia.com/manic/open.html

■ **Microsoft/Vatican Humor**
www.amdahl.com/internet/events/
ms-vatican-text.html

■ **Migraine Boy**
www.migraineboy.com/

■ **Not in My Backyard**
www.notinmybackyard.com/strips/

■ **Onion**
www.theonion.com/

■ **Short Attention Span**
www.amused.com/sass.html

■ **Smile**
www.sacbee.com/smile/smile.html

■ **Stress Relief Aquarium**
www.amused.com/fish.html

▲ www.amused.com/fish.html

■ **Top Cow**
www.topcow.com/

I Can't Keep Staying Up All Night

If you enter one of these sites, you won't leave soon. Consider yourself warned.

■ **Addicted to Stuff**
www.morestuff.com/

■ **After Dinner**
www.afterdinner.com/

■ **Bingo Blitz**
www.worldvillage.com/bingo/index.html

■ **Chains**
found.cs.nyu.edu/andruid/CHAINS.html

■ **Cherry Coke Wall**
www.ccwall.com/

■ **Cold Case**
www.coldcase.com/

■ **Cypher**
www.won.net/gamerooms/rpg/cypher/

■ **Dear Abby**
www.uexpress.com/ups/abby/

■ **Deoxyribonucleic Hyperdimension**
www.deoxy.org/index.htm

■ **Function**
www.function.org/

■ **Greatest Conspiracies**
www.webcom.com/~conspire

■ **History of the Mystery**
www.mysterynet.com/history/mystery/

■ **HotAIR**
www.improb.com/

■ **Infiltration**
www.infiltration.org/

■ **Insomnia**
ccwf.cc.utexas.edu/~swilson/Insomnia.html

■ **Interesting Ideas**
www.mcs.net/~billsw/home.html

■ **Mystery Science Theater 3000**
www.scifi.com/mst3000/

■ **Optical Illusions**
www.sandlotscience.com/

■ **Questioned Document Examination**
www.webmasters.net/qde/

■ **Random Links**
www.random.com/

■ **Synthetic Journal**
www-personal.umich.edu/~rmutt/sj/
index.html

■ **The Case**
www.thecase.com

■ **Trivia Web**
www.trivia.net/

■ **Web Soup**
www.ursus.net/WebSoup/ws.html

■ **What They Meant to Say Was . . .**
www.carpedrm.com/wtmtsw.htm

Information You Probably Don't Need

But we include it anyway, just in case.

■ **Advertising Graveyard**
www.zeldman.com/ad.html

■ **Antics**
www.ionet.net/~rdavis/antics.shtml

■ **Ask Mr. Bad Advice**
www.echonyc.com/~spingo/Mr.BA/

■ **Billy Bob Teeth**
www.billybobteeth.com/

■ **Bodyguard Home Page**
www.iapps.org/

■ **Demotivation Posters**
www.cs.wustl.edu/~schmidt/
demotivation.html

■ **Driveways of the Rich and Famous**
www.driveways.com/

■ **Duct Tape Site**
www.octane.com/ducttape.html

■ **Firewalking**
heartfire.com/firewalk/homefire.html

■ **HQ2O**
www.hq2o.com/

■ **Online Surgery**
www.onlinesurgery.com/

■ **Quitting with Style**
www.iquit.org/

■ **Random Elizabethan Curse Generator**
www.tower.org/insult/insult.html

■ **Shuffle Brain**
www.indiana.edu/~pietsch/

■ **Skeptics Society**
www.skeptic.com/

■ **Sleep Analysis**
www.swoon.com/dream/

■ **Swiss Banks Directory**
www.swconsult.ch/chbanks/index.html

■ **Twinkies**
www.owlnet.rice.edu/~gouge/twinkies.html

■ **Useless Facts**
www.useless-facts.com/

■ **Useless Knowledge**
www.uselessknowledge.com/

■ **Wacky Patent of the Month**
colitz.com/site/wacky.htm

■ **Worldwide Institute for the Preservation of Everything**
www.dungeon.com/~weaver/

■ **Zen Stories to Tell Your Neighbors**
www.rider.edu/users/suler/zenstory/zenstory.html

International Trade

Even business neophytes can get info about international commerce from the Internet.

■ **Europa**
europa.eu.int/index.htm

■ **Global Commerce Link**
www.commerce.com/

■ **Global Trade Center**
www.tradezone.com/welcome.html

■ **Import-Export Portal**
www.fita.org/webindex.html

■ **International Business Forum**
www.ibf.com/

■ **International Business Resources on the WWW**
ciber.bus.msu.edu/busres/inttrade.htm

■ **International Trade Data Network**
www.itdn.net/

■ **Internationalist**
www.internationalist.com/

■ **Investigative Resources International**
www.lainet.com/factfind/

■ **I-Trade**
sys1.tpusa.com/

■ **Trade Compass**
www.tradecompass.com/

■ **Tradeport**
tradeport.org/

■ **U.S. International Trade Commission**
www.usitc.gov/

■ **U.S. International Trade Statistics**
www.census.gov/foreign-trade/www/

■ **U.S. Trade Representative**
www.ustr.gov/

■ **World Trade Center**
www.worldtradecenter.org/

■ **Worldclass Supersite**
web.idirect.com/~tiger/supersit.htm

Internet—Beginners Start Here

Surf smarter. You won't feel like a newbie once you have perused some of these sites.

■ **Beginner's Guide to URLs**
zeppo.ncsa.uiuc.edu/demoweb/
url-primer.html

■ **Beginners Central**
www.northernwebs.com/bc/

▲ www.northernwebs.com/bc/

■ **Best Internet Tutorials**
www.bgsu.edu/departments/tcom/tutors2.html

■ **Butterfly Glossary**
www.rirr.cnuce.cnr.it/Glossario/
glhpage.html

■ **Dummies Daily**
www.dummiesdaily.com/

■ **GettingStarted**
www.gettingstarted.net/

■ **Internet 101**
www2.famvid.com/i101/

■ **Internet Background and Basics**
www.refstar.com/internet/

■ **Internet Dictionary**
www.oh-no.com/define.html

■ **Internet Facts and Stats**
www.parallaxweb.com/interfacts.html

■ **Internet FAQs**
www.boutell.com/faq/

■ **Internet Help Desk**
w3.one.net/~alward/

■ **Internet in a Baby**
www.wideweb.com/baby

■ **Internet Learners**
www.clark.net/pub/lschank/web/learn.html

■ **Learn the Net**
www.learnthenet.com/

■ **Life on the Internet**
www.screen.com/start/welcome.html

■ **Net Lingo**
www.netlingo.com/

■ **Newbie Net**
www.newbie.net/

■ **Overview of the Web**
www.imagescape.com/helpweb/www/
oneweb.html

■ **The Net Minute—Internet Tips**
www.netminute.com/

■ **Web Introduction**
www.cba.uiuc.edu/system/webintro.html

■ **WebNovice**
www.webnovice.com/

■ **WhatIs**
whatis.com/

■ **World Wide Web for the Clueless**
www.mit.edu:8001/people/rei/
wwwintro.html

Internet Directories and Portals

*Good starting places. Just about everything, usu-
ally by category.*

■ **AllCampus**
www.allcampus.com/

■ **Big Eye**
www.bigeye.com

■ **Britannica Internet Guide**
www.britannica.com/

■ **CNET**
www.cnet.com/

■ **Daily Overlook**
www.thedaily.com/overlook.html

■ **Essential Links**
www.el.com/

■ **Galaxy**
www.einet.net/

■ **HotSheet**
www.tstimpreso.com/hotsheet/

■ **Infomine**
lib-www.ucr.edu/Main.html

■ **Infospace**
www.infospace.com/

■ **Link Exchange**
www.linkexchange.com/

■ **LookSmart**
www.looksmart.com

■ **Mining Company**
www.miningco.com/

■ **MyLook**
mylook.com/

■ **NetGuide Live**
www.netguide.com/

■ **Search Beat**
www.search-beat.com/

■ **Snap**
www.snap.com/

■ **Starting Point**
www.stpt.com/

■ **Starwave**
www.starwave.com/

■ **Third Voice**
www.thirdvoice.com/

▲ www.thirdvoice.com/

■ **Virtual Reference Desk**
www.refdesk.com/

■ **Web Soup**
www.ursus.net/WebSoup/

■ **WebCrawler Select**
webcrawler.com/select/

■ **World 1000**
www.hitbox.com/wc/world.html

■ **Yahoo**
www.yahoo.com/

■ **Yanoff's Internet Services**
sirius.we.lc.ehu.es/internet/
inet.services.html

Internet Ethics

These sites include everything from appropriate behavior on the Internet to deep thoughts about its implications for society.

■ **Code of Ethics for Internet E-Commerce**
emailausonline.com.au/auson/ethics.htm

■ **Code of Ethics for Marketing on the Internet**
www.resourcegrp.com/
code_of_ethics_for_marketing_on_.htm

■ **Computer Professionals for Social Responsibility**
snyside.sunnyside.com/home.html/

■ **Cyber Rights**
www.cpsr.org/cpsr/nii/cyber-rights/

■ **Electronic Frontier Foundation**
www.eff.org/

■ **Ethics and the Internet**
www.duke.edu/~wgrobin/ethics/

■ **Ethics of Journalism on the Internet**
userwww.sfsu.edu/~sonlu/topic1.htm

■ **Ethics Resources on the WWW**
www.ethics.ubc.ca/resources/

■ **Internet Behavior and Ethics**
www.abacon.com/compsite/conversation/
netiquette.html

■ **Internet Ethics and Etiquette**
www.ciolek.com/WWWVLPages/QltyPages/
QltyEtiq.html

■ **Internet Ethics Organizations**
www.uncwil.edu/people/vetterr/CLASSES/
csc105-ss98/ethics2.html

■ **Internet Society**
www.isoc.org/

■ **LegalEthics: The Internet Ethics Site**
www.legalethics.com/index.html

■ **Netiquette Home Page**
www.albion.com/netiquette/index.html

■ **Netiquette Primer**
jade.wabash.edu/wabnet/info/netiquet.htm

■ **Phish Net Netiquette**
www.newbie.net/CyberCourse/

■ **Selected Internet Ethics Resources**
www.unf.edu/library/guides/ethics.html

Internet—Everything You've Always Wanted to Know

Potpourri. There are always many Internet-related sites that are hard to categorize.

■ **1001 Internet Tips**
www4.zdnet.com/pccomp/besttips/

■ **Ask Dr. Internet**
promo.net/drnet/

■ **Balkanization of the Web**
www.dsiegel.com/balkanization/

■ **BrowserWatch**
browserwatch.internet.com/

■ **CERN Welcome**
www.cern.ch/

■ **City of Bits**
www-mitpress.mit.edu/City_of_Bits

■ **ColorMix**
www.colormix.com/

■ **Create Your Own Logo**
www.webgfx.ch/

■ **Creative Good Help Pages**
www.creativegood.com/help/index.html

■ **DLL Archive**
solo.abac.com/dllarchive/index.html

■ **Don't Spread That Hoax!**
www.crew.umich.edu/~chymes/newusers/
Think.html

■ **EarthCam**
www.earthcam.com/

■ **Easter Egg Archive**
www.eeggs.com/

■ **File Formats**
www.learnthenet.com/english/html/
34filext.htm

■ **Global Internet Statistics**
www.euromktg.com/globstats/

■ **Hipbone**
www.conavigator.com/

■ **How to Get Your Own Domain Name**
www.cnet.com/Content/Features/Howto/
Domain/

■ **ICYouSee**
www.ithaca.edu/library/Training/
ICYouSee.html#7

■ **Internet Archive**
www.archive.org/

■ **Internet Channel**
www.inch.com/index.html

■ **Internet Economy**
www.internetindicators.com/

■ **Internet Font Browser**
cuiwww.unige.ch/OSG/Fonts/

■ **Internet Information Center**
www.Austria.Eu.Net/iic/

■ **Internet Statistics**
lcweb.loc.gov/global/internet/
inet-stats.html

■ **Internet Web Text Index**
www.december.com/web/text/index.html

■ **Net.Genesis**
www.netgen.com/

■ **Press Questions to Tim Berners-Lee**
www.w3.org/People/Berners-Lee/FAQ.html

■ **Ribbon Campaigns on the Internet**
gargaro.com/ribbons.html

■ **SquareOne Technology**
www.squareonetech.com/

■ **Survey Net**
www.survey.net/

■ **The Rail**
www.therail.com/cgi-bin/station

■ **TUCOWS**
www.tucows.com/

■ **Virtual Tourist World Map**
wings.buffalo.edu/world/

■ **W3C**
www.w3.org/

■ **Web Browsers OpenFAQ**
raq002.aa.net/openfaq/browsers/

■ **Web Developer's Virtual Library**
wdvl.com/

■ **Web Manage Technology**
www.webmanage.com/

■ **Web Monkey**
www.hotwired.com/webmonkey/

■ **Web Rings**
www.webring.org/

■ **Web Standards Project**
www.webstandards.org/

■ **Webopaedia**
webopedia.internet.com/

■ **WebTrends**
www.webtrends.com/

■ **What's New Too!**
newtoo.manifest.com/

■ **World Wide Web Acronyms**
www.ucc.ie/info/net/acronyms/acro.html

■ **World Wide Web Consortium**
www.w3.org/pub/WWW/

■ **WWW Security FAQs**
www-genome.wi.mit.edu/WWW/faqs/
www-security-faq.html

■ **Yahoo What's New**
www.yahoo.com/new

Internet Filters

Filter software can act as a barrier between children and inappropriate sites.

■ **Clean Surf**
www.cleansurf.com/

■ **CyberPatrol**
www.cyberpatrol.com/

■ **Integrity Online**
www.integrityonline16.com/

■ **Internet Filters**
www.solidoak.com/download.htm

■ **Internet Lifeguard**
www.safesurf.com/lifegard.htm

■ **Kid Safety**
www.ou.edu/oupd/kidsafe/inet.htm

■ **Net Nanny**
www.netnanny.com/

■ **Safe for Kids**
www.weburbia.com/pg/safety.htm

■ **SafeSurf**
www.safesurf.com/

Internet Greeting Cards

*Several sites let you send free electronic greeting
cards, often complete with music, to friends online.
The URL for the greeting card site will be waiting
when the recipient picks up his or her e-mail.*

■ **123Greetings**
www.123greetings.com/

■ **Absolutely Amazing Greeting Cards**
microimg.com/postcards/

■ **American Greetings**
www.americangreetings.com/

■ **Blue Mountain**
www1.bluemountain.com/

■ **CardCentral**
www.cardcentral.net/weekly.htm

■ **E-Greetings**
www.egreetings.com/e-products/m_main/
cgi/homepage

■ **Electric Postcard**
postcards.www.media.mit.edu/Postcards/

■ **Hallmark**
www.hallmark.com/

■ **MaxRacks**
www.maxracks.com/

■ **Postcards from the Web**
homearts.com/postcard/00postf1.htm

■ **Send a Greeting**
www.sendgreeting.com/

■ **Web Cards**
www.wbwebcards.com/

Internet History

Pick any one and it should be sufficient. But if the Internet is a passion, then by all means take a look at several.

■ **A Brief History of the Internet**
info.isoc.org/internet-history/brief.html

■ **A Little History of the World Wide Web**
www.w3.org/History.html

■ **About the World Wide Web**
www.w3.org/WWW/

■ **As We May Think**
www.ps.uni-sb.de/~duchier/pub/vbush/
vbush.shtml

■ **Brief History of the Internet and Related Networks**
info.isoc.org/internet-history/cerf.html

■ **Brief History of the Internet**
www0.delphi.com/navnet/faq/history.html

■ **Classic RAND Papers on Packet Switching**
www.rand.org/publications/RM/
baran.list.html

■ **Community Memory**
memex.org/community-memory.html

■ **Digital Time Capsule**
mitsloan.mit.edu/timecapsule/main.html

■ **History of ARPANet**
www.dei.isep.ipp.pt/docs/arpa.html

■ **History of the Internet**
www.internetvalley.com/intval.html

■ **Hobbes Internet Timeline**
info.isoc.org/guest/zakon/Internet/History/
HIT.html

■ **How the Internet Came to Be**
www.bell-labs.com/user/zhwang/vcerf.html

■ **Internet and World Wide Web History**
www.elsop.com/wrc/h_web.htm

■ **Internet Archive**
www.archive.org/

■ **Internet Pioneers**
www.internet-history.org/

■ **Nerds 201: A Brief History of the Internet**
www.pbs.org/opb/nerds2.0.1/

■ **Net Hype**
jrowse.mtx.net/net/hype.html

■ **NetHistory**
www.geocities.com/SiliconValley/2260/

■ **PBS Life on the Internet Timeline**
www.pbs.org/internet/timeline/index.html

■ **Roads and Crossroads of Internet History**
www.internetvalley.com/intvalold.html

■ **Tim Berners-Lee**
www.w3.org/People/Berners-Lee/

■ **Usenet History**
www.vrx.net/usenet/history/

■ **Web Origins and Beyond**
www.seas.upenn.edu/~lzeltser/WWW/

Internet Search Engines

No two search engines are alike. Each has its own attractions and method of presenting results. Try several. You will probably find two or three favorites for your everyday search needs.

■ **Accufind**
www.accufind.com/

■ **All-in-one**
www.albany.net/allinone/all1www.html/
#WWW

■ **AltaVista**
www.altavista.com

■ **Ask Jeeves**
www.ask.com/

■ **Deja News**
www.dejanews.com/

■ **Direct Hit**
www.directhit.com/

■ **Easy Searcher**
www.easysearcher.com/home.html

■ **Editorial Search**
www.opinion-pages.org/

■ **Event Search**
www.ipworld.com/events/search.htm

■ **Excite!**
www.excite.com/

■ **Fast Search**
www.alltheweb.com/

■ **Findspot**
www.findspot.com/

■ **Forum One**
www.forumone.com/

■ **Google**
www.google.com/

▲ www.google.com/

■ **GovBot**
ciir2.cs.umass.edu/Govbot/

■ **HotBot**
www.hotbot.com/

■ **Infoseek**
www.infoseek.com/

■ **Internet Exploration**
www.amdahl.com/internet/

■ **Internet Sleuth**
www.isleuth.com/

■ **Magellan**
www.mckinley.com

■ **MetaCrawler**
www.go2net.com/search.html

■ **NetSearcher**
www.searchinsider.com/

■ **One Look Dictionary**
www.onelook.com/

■ **Philosophy Research**
noesis.evansville.edu/

■ **SearchIQ**
www.searchiq.com/

■ **SportSearch**
www.sportsearch.com/

■ **WebCrawler**
www.webcrawler.com/

Internet Security and Privacy

Both expert and amateur Internet users are concerned about security leaks and privacy erosion on the Internet. These issues are addressed repeatedly by everyone from sociologists to computer scientists. We list some of the easy-to-read sites here.

■ **Anonymity and Privacy on the Internet**
www.stack.nl/~galactus/remailers/

■ **Computer and Internet Security**
lcweb.loc.gov/global/internet/security.html

■ **Computer Security Information**
www.alw.nih.gov/Security/security.html

■ **Cookie Central**
www.cookiecentral.com

■ **Electronic Privacy Information Center**
epic.org/

■ **Georgetown Internet Privacy Policy Study**
www.msb.edu/faculty/culnanm/
gippshome.html

■ **Internet Hoaxes**
ciac.llnl.gov/ciac/CIACHoaxes.html

■ **Internet Privacy Coalition**
www.crypto.org/

■ **Internet Privacy Home Page**
www.osu.edu/units/law/swire1/pspriv.htm

■ **Internet Privacy Sites**
www.cs.buffalo.edu/~milun/privacy.html

■ **Internet Privacy: A Public Concern**
www.research.att.com/~lorrie/pubs/
networker-privacy.html

■ **Internet Scambusters**
www.scambusters.org/index.html

■ **Internet Security Issues and Answers**
www.alw.nih.gov/Security/security.html

■ **Junkbusters**
www.junkbusters.com/

■ **Pretty Good Privacy Help Page**
www.research.umbc.edu/pgp/pgpmain.html

■ **Pretty Good Privacy Presentation**
www.stanford.edu/group/tdr-security/
PGP-Demo/index.htm

■ **Privacy Pages**
www.orlandomaildrop.com/privacy.html

■ Protecting Your Internet Privacy
cc.uoregon.edu/privacy.html

■ The Big Cookie
www.collegehill.com/ilp-news/lide.html

■ TRUSTe
www.etrust.org/

■ Understanding Net Users' Attitudes about Online Privacy
www.research.att.com/projects/
privacystudy/

■ WWW Security FAQs
www.w3.org/Security/Faq/
www-security-faq.html

Internet Service Providers

We will not list all the ISPs who offer their services; that is what these comprehensive sites do.

■ Directory of ISPs
thedirectory.org/index.sht

■ Guide to Finding a Decent ISP
dogwolf.seagull.net/

■ Internet Access Providers Metalist
www.herbison.com/herbison/
iap_meta_list.html

■ ISP Finder
www.cleansurf.com/

■ NetAccess Worldwide
www.netalert.com/

■ **The List: ISPs**
thelist.iworld.com/

■ **Ultimate Guide to ISPs**
www.cnet.com/Content/Reviews/Compare/ISP/

Internet Site Makers and Designers

Want to see how the pros do it? Check out the sites these designers make for themselves. Then check out the sites for their clientele.

■ **4site**
4site.co.il/

■ **47Jane**
www.47jane.com/

■ **A List Apart**
www.alistapart.com/

■ **Accent Design**
www.accentdesign.com/

■ **Adjacency**
www.adjacency.com/

■ **Adscape**
www.adscape.com/

■ **Aristotle**
www.aristotle.net/design

■ **Black Box**
www.theblackbox.com/

■ **Blue Cat Design**
www.bluecatdesign.com/

■ **Blueberry**
www.blueberry.co.uk/

■ **Brody**
www.brodynewmedia.com/

■ **Chman**
www.chman.com/

■ **Curry Design**
www.currydesign.com/

■ **CyberNation**
www.cnation.com

■ **Dahlin Smith White**
www.dsw.com

■ **Dan Design**
www.his.com/~dan/

■ **Design Project**
design-agency.com/project/

■ **EasyNet France**
www.easynet.fr

■ **Eclectica**
www.the-eclectica.com/contents.htm

■ **Egomedia**
www.egomedia.com

■ **EYE4U**
www.eye4u.com/

■ **Fire Engine Red**
www.enginered.com/

- **Gabocorp**
www.gabocorp.com/
- **Giant Step**
www.giantstep.com/
- **Green Ant**
www.greenant.com.au/
- **Hi-D**
www.hi-d.com/
- **Hillman Curtis**
www.hillmancurtis.com/
- **I2F**
www.i2f.org/
- **Ignition**
www.ignitiondesign.com/index.html
- **Ikonic**
www.ikonic.com/
- **Ingram Labs**
www.ingramlabs.com/
- **Internet Professional Publishers**
www.ippa.org/
- **Jiong**
www.jiong.com/
- **John Hersey**
www.hersey.com/
- **Juxt Interactive**
www.juxtinteractive.com/
- **K2 Design**
www.k2design.com/

■ **Magnet Interactive**
www.magnet.com/

■ **NetArchitects**
www.netarchitects.com/

■ **Nofrontiere**
www.nofrontiere.com/

■ **Oden**
www.odenvision.com/

■ **Off the Page Productions**
www.offthepage.com/

■ **Organic Online**
www.organic.com/

■ **OS Web Creations**
www.os-web.com/

■ **P2 Output**
www.p2output.com/

■ **Page 2 Design**
home.eznet.net/~tia69kis/page_2_design/

■ **Phoenix Pop**
www.3pdesign.com/

■ **Plexus Web Creations**
www.plexusweb.com/

■ **Primo Angeli**
www.primo.com/

■ **Project Cool Media**
www.projectcool.com/

■ **Prophet Communications**
www.prophetcomm.com/

- **Razorfish**
www.razorfish.com/

- **Robbie de Villiars Design**
robbie.com/

- **Scroll**
scroll.behaviour.com/toc/toc.html

- **Second Story**
www.secondstory.com/

- **Shadowmaker**
www.shadowboxer.com/

- **Sharp Services**
www.sharp-ideas.com/sharp.html

- **Siteline**
www.siteline.com/

- **Souldanse Digital Design**
www.souldanse.com/

- **Speared Peanut**
www.spearedpeanut.com/

- **Studio1**
www.studio1.com.au/penstrokes/

- **Superbad**
www.superbad.com

- **Systems Alliance**
www.systemsalliance.com/index.cfm

- **Talbot Design**
www.talbotdesign.com/

- **Taylor and Pond**
www.taylorpond.com/

■ **Twelve Point Rule**
www.fusebox.com/

■ **Verso**
www.verso.com/

■ **Virtual Light Media**
www.virtuallightmedia.com/

■ **Vivid Studios**
www.vivid.com/

■ **VolumeOne**
www.volumeone.com/

Internet Webmasters

If you want to be a webmaster, or just wonder what they do, these sites supply plenty of information.

■ **20 Tips for Mac Webmasters**
www.clearway.com/team/clearway/
mac-web-tips/home.html

■ **Fade In, Fade Out**
builder.com/Authoring/MoreStupid/ss01.
html

■ **International Webmasters Association**
www.irwa.org/

■ **Professor Pete's Webmastering 301**
www.professorpete.com/

■ **Webmaster Seminars**
www.webmasterseminars.com/

■ **Webmaster's Guide to Search Engines**
searchenginewatch.com/wgtse.htm

■ **Webmaster's Notebook**
www.cio.com/forums/intranet/notebook.html

■ **Webmaster Association**
www.stars.com/Internet/Web/Associations.html

■ **Webmastery**
www.nothing.com/webmastery/

■ **Webmaster Central**
webvivre.hypermart.net/

■ **Webmaster International**
www.webmasterint.com/index5.htm

■ **Webmaster Reference Library**
www.webreference.com/

■ **Webmaster Station**
www.exeat.com/index.shtml

■ **Webmaster Territory**
www-scf.usc.edu/~bako/webmaster/non-java.html

■ **Webmaster's Color Lab**
www.visibone.com/colorlab/

■ **Webmaster's Guild**
www.thedaily.washington.edu/staff/martin/webmasters.guild/

Internships

We hope this list is helpful. However, most people get internships locally through networking.

■ **College Internships 101**
members.aol.com/marineraid/index.html

■ **D.C. Internships**
www.dclrs.com/intern.htm

■ **Holocaust Museum Internships**
www.ushmm.org/internship.htm

■ **International Internships**
darkwing.uoregon.edu/~isp/internships/
jobs-internships.html

■ **Internship Hotline**
www.internhotline.com/

■ **Internships and Fieldwork Nationwide**
minerva.acc.virginia.edu/~career/intern.html

■ **Internships Directory**
www.feminist.org/911/internship/
internship.html

■ **Internships Tokyo**
jintern.com/

■ **Lands' End Internships**
de.landsend.com/

■ **Mighty Internship Review**
www.daily.umn.edu/~mckinney/

■ **National Internships**
campus.net/busemp/nintern/

■ **National Interships Online**
www.internships.com/

■ **PBS Jobs and Internships**
www.pbs.org/insidepbs/jobs/

■ **Rising Star Internships**
www.rsinternships.com/

■ **SHAPE Internship Center**
www.mindquest.bloomington.k12.mn.us/
intern/

■ **Small Business
Administration Internships**
www.sba.gov/pmi/

■ **Smithsonian Internships**
www.si.edu/youandsi/studies/infell.htm

■ **Sources of Internships**
www.brandeis.edu/hiatt/web_data/
internships.html

■ **Summer Jobs, Internships**
www.jobweb.org/catapult/jintern.htm

■ **Television Student Internships**
www.moviebytes.com/mb_contest_detail.
cfm?contestnumber=1

■ **Tripod Internships**
www.tripod.com/explore/jobs_career/
internships.html

■ **Washington Center Internships**
www.twc.edu/

■ **Washington Intern Foundation**
interns.org/

Java

OK, you've heard about it. But just what is it? And how can you use it? These sites tell all.

■ **Brewing Java: A Tutorial**
metalab.unc.edu/javafaq/javatutorial.html

■ **Club Java**
rendezvous.com/java/

■ **Cobb's Obligatory Java**
www.ccobb.org/javalinks.html

■ **Coffee Break**
www.davidreilly.com/jcb/

■ **ColorCenter**
www.hidaho.com/colorcenter/

■ **Digital Espresso**
www.mentorsoft.com/DE/

■ **Gamelan: Programming in Java**
www.gamelan.com/

■ **Introduction to Java**
www.ibm.com/java/education/intro/
courseoptions.htm

■ **Java Exhibition**
www.euroyellowpages.com/exhibitn/
javahome.html

■ **Java FAQ Archives**
www-net.com/java/faq/

- **Java FAQs**
  java.sun.com/products/jdk/faq.html
- **Java Home Page**
  java.sun.com/
- **Java Q & A**
  steggy.minn.net/~psmith/qa.html
- **Java Readings and Resources**
  www.unc.edu/cit/guides/irg-42.html
- **Java Samples**
  199.18.35.104/java/java.html
- **Java Software**
  www.stars.com/Software/Java/
- **Java Tutorial**
  java.sun.com/nav/read/Tutorial/
- **JavaWorld Magazine**
  www.javaworld.com/
- **Making Sense of Java**
  www.disordered.org/Java-QA.html
- **Presenting Java**
  www.december.com/works/java.html
- **Sun's Listing of Java Books**
  www.sun.com/javabooks/

Journalism

Journalism sites range from resources for getting the story to staunch defenses of the right to report the story.

■ **Associated Press Managing Editors**
www.apme.com/

■ **CNN Search**
www.cnn.com/SEARCH/index.html

■ **Committee to Protect Journalists**
www.cpj.org/

■ **Digital Journalist**
dirckhalstead.org/

■ **Experts Directory**
www.experts.com/

■ **Experts, Authorities,
and Spokespersons**
www.yearbooknews.com/

■ **Freedom Forum**
www.freedomforum.org/

■ **Internet Newsroom**
www2.dgsys.com/~editors/

■ **Journalism History**
www.mediahistory.com/journ.html

■ **Mediamatic Index**
www.mediamatic.nl/index.html

■ **National Press Club**
npc.press.org/

■ **Native Americans
Journalists Association**
www.medill.nwu.edu/naja/

■ **Online Journalism Review**
www.ojr.org/

■ **Photojournalist's Coffeehouse**
www.intac.com/~jdeck/index2.html

■ **Plesser Associates**
www.plesser.com/

■ **Pulitzer Prizes**
www.pulitzer.org/

■ **Spot for Copyeditors**
www.theslot.com/

■ **Young Media Professionals**
www.accessabc.com/ympc/ympmedia.html

Kid Stuff

We could fill this whole book with nothing but child-oriented sites. Some are educational but most are just entertaining. Here are the best picks.

■ **10-Minute Bedtime Tour**
www.hamstertours.com/

■ **Alex's Box of Crayons**
www.kidalex.com/

■ **Ask Dr. Universe**
www.wsu.edu/DrUniverse/

■ **Bonus**
www.bonus.com/

■ **Booville**
usacitylink.com/boo/main.html

■ **ChaosKids**
chaoskids.com/

■ **Club-Z**
www.club-z.com/

■ **Cool Science for Curious Kids**
www.hhmi.org/coolscience/

■ **Dinosaur Eggs**
www.quaker-dinoeggs.com/

■ **Kid's Castle**
www.kidscastle.si.edu/

■ **Kids' Almanac**
kids.infoplease.com/

■ **Lego Mindstorm**
www.legomindstorms.com

■ **Lego**
www.lego.com/

■ **Lemonade Stand**
www.littlejason.com/lemonade/

■ **Mr. Rogers' Neighborhood**
www.pbs.org/rogers/

■ **Mudball**
mudball.com/

■ **National Spelling Bee**
www.spellingbee.com/

■ **Newton's Apple**
ericir.syr.edu/Projects/Newton/

■ **Nickelodeon**
www.nick.com

■ **Non-Stick Looney Page**
www.nonstick.com/

■ **Planet Troll**
www.troll.com/

■ **Sandlot Science**
www.sandlotscience.com/

■ **Shooter's Doghouse**
www.shooterdog.com/

■ **Sports Illustrated for Kids**
www.sikids.com/

■ **Sticker World**
www.ctw.org/stickerworld/

■ **Stories to Grow By**
www.storiestogrowby.com/

■ **T Rex**
www.imax.com/t-rex/

■ **Theodore Tugboat**
www.cochran.com/theodore/

■ **Too Cool for Grownups**
www.tcfg.com/

■ **Willie Wonka**
www.wonka.com/Home/wonka_home.html

■ **World Kids**
www.worldkids.com/

■ **Yahooligans**
www.yahooligans.com/

■ **Yeeeoww!**
www.yeeeoww.com/
■ **Zoom Dinosaurs**
www.zoomdinosaurs.com/

Law—Forensic Science

Forensic science means "science as it relates to law"—usually the science involved in solving a crime.

■ **American Academy of Forensic Psychology**
www.abfp.com/
■ **American Society of Forensic Odontology**
asfo.org/
■ **Computer Forensics**
www.forensics.com/
■ **Forensic Entomology**
www.forensic-entomology.com/
■ **Forensic Links**
www.see-incorp.com/links.html
■ **Forensic Science Center**
hyperion.advanced.org/17133/forindex.html
■ **Reddy's Forensic Home Page**
haven.ios.com/~nyrc/homepage.html

■ **The True Witness**
library.advanced.org/17049/gather/

Law—General

*Need help with legal research? Just need help?
Legal matters, large and small, are addressed on
many sites.*

■ **American Bar Association**
www.abanet.org/home.html

■ **Anatomy of a Murder**
tqd.advanced.org/2760/

■ **Bazelon Center for Mental
Health Law**
www.bazelon.org/

■ **Crime Statistics**
www.ojp.usdoj.gov/bjs/

■ **Critical Criminology**
sun.soci.niu.edu/~critcrim/

■ **Cyberjury**
www.cyberjury.com/

■ **DivorceNet**
www.divorcenet.com/

■ **Dumb Laws**
www.dumblaws.com/

■ **Employment Law Resource Center**
www.ahipubs.com/

■ **Famous American Trials**
www.law.umkc.edu/faculty/projects/Ftrials/
ftrials.htm

■ **Federal Judicial Center**
www.fjc.gov/

■ **FedLaw**
www.legal.gsa.gov/

■ **Hieros Gamos**
www.hg.org/

■ **Immigration Lawyers on the Web**
ilw.com/

■ **International Constitutional Law**
www.uni-wuerzburg.de/law/index.html

■ **Justice Information Center**
www.ncjrs.org/

■ **Law Engine**
www.fastsearch.com/law/

■ **Law Forum**
www.lawforum.net/

■ **Law News Network**
www.lawnewsnetwork.com/

■ **Law.com**
www.law.com/

■ **LawGuru**
www.lawguru.com/

- **LawWorld**
www.lawworld.com/
- **Legal Information Institute**
www.law.cornell.edu/
- **Litigation Site**
www.ljx.com/litigation/
- **Police Dogs**
www.policek9.com/
- **Prairie Law**
prairielaw.com/
- **Southern Poverty Law Center**
www.splcenter.org/
- **The Courthouse**
www.ljextra.com/courthouse/
- **U.S. Supreme Court Decisions**
supct.law.cornell.edu/supct/
- **United States Code**
www4.law.cornell.edu/uscode/
- **Virtual Magistrate**
vmag.vcilp.org/

Law—Intellectual Property

Intellectual property is of particular interest to users of the Internet.

- **Free Trade Area for the Americas**
www.cptech.org/pharm/belopaper.html

■ **Intellectual Property and Technology Forum**
infoeagle.bc.edu/bc_org/avp/law/st_org/ipg/iptf/

■ **Intellectual Property Center**
www.ipcenter.com/

■ **Intellectual Property Data Collections**
ipdl.wipo.int/

■ **Intellectual Property Law Server**
www.intelproplaw.com/

■ **Intellectual Property Law Web Server**
www.patents.com/

■ **Intellectual Property: Copyrights, Trademarks, & Patents**
www.brint.com/IntellP.htm

■ **Patent, Trademark, and Copyright Information and Search**
pw1.netcom.com/~patents2/thefirm.html

■ **Patent, Trademark, Copyright World**
www.ptcworld.com/

■ **U.S. House of Representatives Internet Law Library**
law.house.gov/105.htm

■ **U.S. Intellectual Property for Non-lawyers**
www.fplc.edu/tfield/order.htm

Maps

Most of the maps offered by these sites are useful and some are even beautiful. But the handiest sites are the ones that draw a map to your specifications. Print it out and start your trip.

■ **Air Quality Mapping**
www.epa.gov/airnow/

■ **Airport Maps**
www.thetrip.com/airport/

■ **Antique Map Fair**
www.AntiqueMaps.co.uk/

■ **Applied Geographics**
www.appgeo.com/

■ **Area Accurate Map**
www.webcom.com/bright/petermap.html

■ **Atlas of Cyberspace**
www.cybergeography.com/

■ **Census Bureau Digital Map Database**
tiger.census.gov/

■ **Color Landform Map of the U.S.**
fermi.jhuapl.edu/states/states.html

■ **DeLorme Mapping**
www.delorme.com/

■ **Etak**
www.etak.com/

■ **Graphic Maps**
www.graphicmaps.com/graphic_maps.html

■ **Historical Atlas of the 20th Century**
www.erols.com/mwhite28/20centry.htm

■ **Historical Maps of the U.S.**
www.lib.utexas.edu/Libs/PCL/
Map_collection/histus.html

■ **History of Cartography**
www-map.lib.umn.edu/
history_of_cartography.html

■ **International Maps**
www.galaxymaps.com/

■ **Library of Congress Map Collections**
memory.loc.gov/ammem/gmdhtml/
gmdhome.html

■ **Lycos RoadMaps**
www.lycos.com/roadmap.html

■ **Map and Compass**
info.er.usgs.gov/fact-sheets/
finding-your-way/finding-your-way.html

■ **MapBlast**
www.mapblast.com/

■ **MapQuest**
www.mapquest.com/

■ **Maps in the News**
www-map.lib.umn.edu/news.html

■ **Maps On Us**
www.mapsonus.com/

■ **National Geographic Map Machine**
www.etak.com/

■ **Open World City Guides**
www.libs.uga.edu/darchive/hargrett/maps/
maps.html

■ **Rand McNally**
www.randmcnally.com/home/

■ **Rare Map Collection**
www.libs.uga.edu/darchive/hargrett/maps/
maps.html

■ **Road Map Collectors of America**
www.roadmaps.org/

■ **Subway Maps**
www.libs.uga.edu/darchive/hargrett/maps/
maps.html

■ **Thomas Brothers Mapping**
www.thomas.com/

■ **U.S. Gazeteer**
www.census.gov/cgi-bin/gazetteer

■ **Volcanic Maps**
www.geo.mtu.edu/volcanoes/world.html

■ **Washington, D.C. Sightseeing Map**
sc94.ameslab.gov/TOUR/tour.html

■ **World City Maps**
www.lib.utexas.edu/Libs/PCL/
Map_collection/world_cities.html

■ **World of Maps**
www.worldofmaps.com/

■ **Xerox PARC MapWeb Server**
pubweb.parc.xerox.com/

Mathematics

Tricks and tips and help with math.

■ **Absurd Math**
www.absurdmath.inter.net/abmath/

■ **Algebra Online**
www.algebra-online.com/

■ **Applied Math Resources**
www.math.rpi.edu/www/appmath.html

■ **Ask Adam**
www.askadam.com/

■ **Ask Dr. Math**
forum.swarthmore.edu/dr.math/

■ **Brain Exerciser**
www.math.tau.ac.il/~puzne/gif/brain.html

■ **Brain Teasers**
www.eduplace.com/math/brain/index.html

■ **E-Math**
e-math.ams.org/

■ **Exploring Your Future in Math and Science**
www.cs.wisc.edu/~karavan/afl/home.html

■ **Fantastic Math Tricks**
www.angelfire.com/me/marmalade/
mathtips.html

■ **Interactive Math**
tqd.advanced.org/2647/index.html

■ **Interactive Mathematics Miscellany and Puzzles**
www.cut-the-knot.com/

■ **Inverse Symbolic Calculator**
www.cecm.sfu.ca/projects/ISC/

■ **Math Baseball**
www.funbrain.com/math/

■ **Math Forum**
forum.swarthmore.edu/

■ **Math Homework Help**
www.erols.com/bram/column2.html

■ **Math in Daily Life**
www.learner.org/exhibits/dailymath/

■ **Math League Help Topics**
www.mathleague.com/help/help.htm

■ **Mathematician Trading Cards**
www.bulletproof.org/math/default.asp

■ **MathSoft**
www.mathsoft.com/

■ **Mega-Mathematics**
www.cs.uidaho.edu/~casey931/mega-math/menu.html

■ **Monster Math**
www.lifelong.com/CarnivalWorld/MonsterMath/MonMathHP.html

■ **Ridiculously Enhanced Pi Page**
www.exploratorium.edu/learning_studio/pi/

■ **Virtual Math Tutoring Center**
www.miracletutoring.com/

■ **WebMath**
www.webmath.com/

Miscellaneous

Don't know where to put these sites, but they are too good to pass up.

■ **50 State Quarters**
www.usmint.gov/50states/

■ **Alcatraz**
www.nps.gov/alcatraz/

■ **Broken Plank**
www.profiles.nlm.nih.gov/

■ **Caricature Zone**
www.magixl.com/

■ **Circlemakers**
www.circlemakers.org/

■ **Curse of a Thousand Chain Letters**
www.personal.psu.edu/users/d/r/drl146/
curses/

■ **Cynic's Sanctuary**
www.amz.com/cynic/

■ **Despair, Inc.**
www.despair.com/

■ **Desperado Roller Coaster**
www.vegaslounge.com/coasters/
desperado.html

■ **Estimated IQs of the Greatest Geniuses**
home8.swipnet.se/~w-80790/Index.htm

■ **Fading Ad Campaign**
www.frankjump.com/

■ **Fake Food**
www.faxfoods.com/

■ **Fifty Things Worth Saving**
www.fiftythings.com/

■ **Grass-roots Heroes**
www.grass-roots.org/

■ **Half a Cow**
www.halfacow.com/

▲ www.halfacow.com/

■ **Her Majesty's Prison Service**
www.hmprisonservice.gov.uk/

■ **I Thee Web**
hollywoodandvine.com/Itheeweb/

■ **Ice Trek**
www.icetrek.org/

■ **Infinite Fish**
infinitefish.com/

■ **Kvetch**
www.kvetch.com/index.html

■ **Laura's NYC Tales**
www.laurasnyctales.com/

■ **Life Raft**
www.liferaft.com/

■ **Mystery of the Day**
www.mysteries.com/

■ **Name That Candybar**
www.sci.mus.mn.us/sln/tf/c/crosssection/
namethatbar.html

■ **New York Underground**
www.nationalgeographic.com/features/97/
nyunderground/index.html

■ **NYCabbie**
www.nycabbie.com/

■ **Odd Facts**
www.telacommunications.com/misc/facts.htm

■ **Open Diary**
www.opendiary.com/

■ **Pogo Sticks**
www.hvnet.com/pogoplaza/

■ **Professional Butlers**
www.butlersguild.com/

- **Sand Monks**
www.nga.gov.au/Whats_New/monks.html
- **Sneaker Nation**
sneaker-nation.com/
- **Spizzerinctum**
www.mcs.net/~kvj/spizz.html
- **Su Tzu's Chinese Philosophy Page**
mars.superlink.net/fsu/
- **The 80s Server**
www.80s.com/
- **The Anomolist**
www.anomalist.com/
- **Traffic Jam Cure**
www.eskimo.com/~billb/amateur/traffic/
seatraf.html
- **Vanity License Plates**
www.vanity-plates.com/
- **Wealthiest Americans**
www.americanheritage.com/98/oct/40index.htm
- **World Birthday Web**
www.boutell.com/birthday.cgi/
- **World Wide Cemetery**
www.interlog.com/~cemetery/

Movies

If movies are your passion, or even if they are not, you can find out anything at all about them on the Internet. This long list is just a small subset of what is available.

■ **AAAFilm**
www.aaafilm.com/

■ **CineMedia**
ptd15.afionline.org/CineMedia/

■ **Cult Films**
sepnet.com/rcramer/tv.htm

■ **Dermatology in the Cinema**
www.skinema.com/

■ **Film Scouts**
www.filmscouts.com/

■ **FilmFour**
www.filmfour.com

■ **Flicker**
www.sirius.com/~sstark

■ **Former Child Star Central**
members.tripod.com/~former_child_star/

■ **From Script to Screen**
fromscript2screen.com/

■ **Hitchcock Page**
www.primenet.com/~mwc/

■ **Hollywood Archeology**
www.echonyc.com/~hwdarch/

■ **IMAX**
www.imax.com/home.shtml

■ **Internet Movie Database**
www.imdb.com

■ **Loew's Cineplex**
www.theatres.sre.sony.com/

■ **MGM**
www.mgmua.com/

■ **Miramax**
www.miramax.com/

■ **Movie Posters**
www.musicman.com/mp/posters.html

■ **Moviefone**
www.moviefone.com/

■ **Quotes from the Movies**
members.tripod.com/adm/popup/
roadmap.shtml

■ **Silent Movies**
www.cs.monash.edu.au/~pringle/silent/

■ **Small Movies**
www.city-net.com/~fodder/

■ **Sundance Film Festival**
plaza.interport.net/festival/

■ **Trailer Awards**
sites.hollywood.com/trailerawards/

■ **Worst Movies on Earth**
www.ohthehumanity.com/

Multimedia Resources

Here are sites that describe multimedia technology and/or sell a multimedia product.

■ **Byron Preiss Multimedia**
www.byronpreiss.com/

■ **Free Multimedia HyperArchive**
directions.simplenet.com/hobbes/
hyperarchive.html

■ **Macromedia**
www.macromedia.com/

■ **MPEG Resources**
www.mpeg.org/index.html/

■ **Multimedia Authoring Web**
www.mcli.dist.maricopa.edu/authoring/

■ **Multimedia Information Sources**
viswiz.gmd.de/MultimediaInfo/

■ **Multimedia Search**
www.scour.net/

■ **RealNetworks**
www.prognet.com/

■ **Voxware**
www.voxware.com/

Multimedia Site Examples

These sites are listed here specifically because they emphasize their use of multimedia products. Expect to see motion and hear sound, or to be nagged to get the software that will let you do it. Note, however, that many sites listed in other categories also use multimedia.

■ **Addicted to Noise**
www.addict.com/

■ **Agi Arbeitsgruppe Internet Stuttgart**
www.agi.de/frames.htm

■ **Akimbo Design**
www.akimbodesign.com/

■ **Alanis Morissette**
www.maverickrc.com/alanis/main.html

■ **Alice's Adventure's in Wonderland**
www.megabrands.com/alice/goalice.html

■ **Andy's Garage Sale**
www.andysgarage.com/

■ **Babylon 5**
www.babylon5.com/cmp/

■ **Big Shot**
www.spe.sony.com/Pictures/tv/bigshot/

■ **Billabong**
www.billabong.com/

■ **BlockBuilder**
www.vizability.com/vizAbil/VizBlBu.htm

■ **Blue Hypermedia**
www.bluehypermedia.com/f3index.html

■ **Candystand**
www.candystand.com

■ **Citizen Kanine**
www.ammg.com/Virtuville/K9/kanine.html

■ **CleverMedia Arcade Games**
clevermedia.com/arcade/

■ **Coca Cola Japan**
www.cocacola.co.jp/down.htm

■ **Colenso**
webnz.com/colenso/

■ **Colgate**
www.colgate.com/Kids-world/Jungle/

■ **Counterspace**
www.studiomotiv.com/counterspace/space.htm

■ **De-Lux'O Land**
www.deluxoland.com/SHOCK.html

■ **Diet Coke**
www.dietcoke.com/

■ **DreamWorks Records**
www.dreamworksrec.com/

■ **Fox Kids Online**
www.foxkids.com/

■ **Frog Design**
www.frogdesign.com

■ **GapKids**
www.gapkids.com/

■ **GNA World**
www.gnaworld.net/

■ **Habanero Computing Solutions**
www.habanero.com/

■ **Halloween Cards**
www.123cards.com/halloween/
animatedcards/index.html

■ **Homewrecker**
www.homewrecker.com/main.html

■ **Hot Wheels**
www.hotwheels.com/speedcity/

■ **HP Spectometer**
chem.external.hp.com/cag/products/
universo_welcome.html

■ **IBM Research Demo**
www.research.ibm.com/research/demos/
gmr/index.html

■ **Lego Tecnic City**
www.lego.com/technic/cybermaster/
cyberscoop.asp

■ **MkzdK**
www.nets.com/mkzdk/

■ **Nestle Ventura**
www.nestleventura.co.uk/index_h.htm

■ **Nike**
www.Nike.com

■ **Pandora Interactive Studio**
www.pandora.com.sg/

■ **Peugeot**
www.peugeot206.co.uk/

■ **Pop Rocket's Shockwave
Game Arena**
www.poprocket.com/welcome.html

■ **Progressive Mobile Electronics**
www.progressivemobile.com/index2.html

■ **Robot Dancer**
www.multimania.com/goprof/
fsdancer.htm

■ **Rockweb**
www.rockweb.com/

■ **Rod Stewart**
www.rodstewartlive.com/mxrodhome.html

■ **Saatchi and Saatchi**
www.saatchi-saatchi.com/

■ **San Francisco Ballet**
www.sfballet.org

■ **Sharp Electronics**
www.sharp-usa.com/FlashOn.asp

■ **Spy Watch**
www.bbc.co.uk/education/lookandread/

■ **Studio Archetype**
www.studioarchetype.com

■ **The Park**
www.the-park.com/

■ **Ultra Lounge**
www.ultralounge.com/

■ **Volvo**
new.car.volvo.com/

■ **Warner Brothers**
www.warnerbros.com/

■ **Wet Cement**
www.lasvegassun.com/sun/dossier/events/
cementkid/game.html

Museums

Actual museums are available in many locales, but those in distant places are now available— and beautifully presented—online.

■ **7th Museum**
www.Desk.nl/~seventh/

■ **All Aboard the Silver Streak**
www.msichicago.org/exhibit/zephyr/

■ **American Museum of Photography**
www.photographymuseum.com/

■ **Andy Warhol Museum**
www.warhol.org/

■ **Bad Fads Museum**
www.adscape.com/badfads/

■ **Cooper-Hewitt National Design Museum**
www.si.edu/ndm/dfl/

■ **de Young**
www.thinker.org/index.shtml

■ **Drop Zone**
www.thedropzone.org/

■ **Exploratorium**
www.exploratorium.edu/

■ **Franklin Institute Virtual Science Museum**
sln.fi.edu/

■ **Guggenheim Museum**
www.guggenheim.org/

■ **Guide to Museums and
Cultural Resources**
www.lam.mus.ca.us/webmuseums/

■ **Hans Christian Andersen Museum**
www.odkomm.dk/int/hcamuk.htm

■ **Henry Ford Museum**
www.hfmgv.org/

■ **Holocaust Museum**
www.mznet.org/chamber/

■ **Holography Museum**
www.holoworld.com/

■ **Hudson River Museum**
www.hrm.org/

■ **Insect Museum**
www.insecta.com/

■ **Isamu Noguchi Museum**
www.noguchi.org/

■ **Israel Museum**
www.imj.org.il/

■ **J. Paul Getty Museum**
www.getty.edu/museum/home.htm

■ **Le Musee de Beaux-Arts**
www.mmfa.qc.ca/

■ **Metropolitan Museum of Art**
www.metmuseum.org/htmlfile/gallery/
gallery.html

■ **Murnau Castle Museum**
www.lrz-muenchen.de/~kl921aa/WWW/
index2.html

■ **Musee Rodin**
www.musee-rodin.fr/

■ **Museum of Antiquities**
www.ncl.ac.uk/~nantiq/

■ **Museum of Surgical Science**
www.imss.org/

■ **Museum of Women's History**
www.nmwh.org/

■ **Museum of Television and Radio**
www.mtr.org/

■ **Natural History Museum**
www.nhm.ac.uk/

■ **Newseum**
www.newseum.org

■ **Obsolete Computer Museum**
www.ncsc.dni.us/fun/user/tcc/cmuseum/
cmuseum.htm

■ **Peabody Museum of Archaeology and Ethnology**
www.peabody.harvard.edu/

■ **Photo Museum**
www.photographymuseum.com/

■ **Smithsonian**
www.si.edu/

■ **Tech Museum of Innovation**
www.thetech.org/
■ **Tenement Museum**
www.wnet.org/tenement/

Music

Can we cover all types of music in this short list? We tried. But if you have an interest not mentioned here, a search engine will probably uncover matching sites.

■ **All-Music Guide**
www.allmusic.com/index.html
■ **Artist Underground**
www.aumusic.com/
■ **Classical Insites**
www.classicalinsites.com/
■ **Classical Net Home Page**
www.classical.net/music/
■ **CountrySong**
www.countrysong.com/
■ **FenderWorld**
www.fender.com/
■ **Gilbert and Sullivan**
diamond.idbsu.edu/gas/GaS.html

■ **Harmony Music List**
www.sdam.com/harmony/

■ **House of Blues**
www.hob.com/

■ **Instrument Encyclopedia**
www.si.umich.edu/CHICO/MHN/
enclpdia.html

■ **International Lyrics Server**
www.lyrics.ch/

■ **Internet Beatles Album**
www.primenet.com/~dhaber/beatles.html

■ **J. S. Bach Home Page**
www.tile.net/tile/bach/index.html

■ **Jazz Online**
www.jazzonln.com/

■ **Knitting Factory**
www.knittingfactory.com/

■ **Metallica**
www.metclub.com/images/qtvr/
index.html

■ **MP3**
www.mp3.com/

■ **MTV Online**
www.mtv.com/

■ **Music in the Public Domain**
www.pdinfo.com/list.htm

■ **MusicSearch**
musicsearch.com/

■ **MyLaunch**
www.mylaunch.com/

■ **Piano on the Net**
www.artdsm.com/music.html

■ **Picklehead Music**
www.picklehead.com/

■ **Pollstar**
www.addict.com/

■ **Ragtime**
www.ragtimers.org/

■ **Red Hot Jazz Archive**
www.redhotjazz.com/

■ **Roadie.net**
www.roadie.net/

■ **Rock and Roll Hall of Fame**
www.rockhall.com

■ **Rocktropolis**
www.rocktropolis.com/

■ **SonicNet**
www.sonicnet.com

■ **Strange and Beautiful Music**
www.strangeandbeautiful.com/

■ **StreetSound**
www.streetsound.com/

■ **Toonman**
www.toonman.com/start.html

■ **Ultimate Band List**
www.ubl.com/

■ **Vibe**
www.vibe.com/

■ **Wall of Sound**
wallofsound.go.com/index.html

■ **Webnoize**
www.webnoize.com/

■ **Young Composers**
www.youngcomposers.com/

Nature

This list is fairly short because most nature-related sites have environmental overtones and have been listed in that category; see also Save the Planet.

■ **Bear Den**
www.nature-net.com/bears/

■ **Butterfly Website**
butterflywebsite.com/awards.htm

■ **Canadian Nature Federation**
www.cnf.ca/

■ **Connecting with Nature**
www.pacificrim.net/~nature/

■ **English Nature**
www.english-nature.org.uk/

■ **GORP Wildlife**
www.gorp.com/gorp/activity/wildlife.htm

■ **Nature and Wildlife Photography**
www.infop.com/photo/

■ **Nature Awareness School**
www.nature.valleyva.com/

■ **Nature Journal**
www.nature.com/

■ **Nature Park Home Page**
www.naturepark.com/

■ **Nature Photo Index**
www.naturepix.com/

■ **Nature Rangers**
www.naturerangers.com/

■ **Nature Smart**
www.naturesmart.com/

■ **Nature's Classroom**
www.naturesclassroom.org/

■ **Second Nature: Education for Sustainability**
www.2nature.org/

■ **Smithsonian Gem and Mineral Collection**
galaxy.einet.net/images/gems/gems-icons.html

■ **Species in the Park**
ice.ucdavis.edu/nps/

■ **Virtual Cave**
www.goodearth.com/virtcave.html

■ **Wild Wings Heading North**
north.audubon.org/

News

Breaking news often shows up on the Internet long before it reaches traditional news media. Beyond that, news reaches a new level of convenience on the Internet: you can take what you want from a great variety of sources.

■ **ABC News**
www.abcnews.com/

■ **AJR NewsLink**
www.newslink.org/

■ **BBC**
www.bbc.co.uk/

■ **Boston Globe**
www.boston.com/globe/

■ **CANOE: Canadian Online Explorer**
www.canoe.ca/

■ **CBS News**
www.cbs.com/

■ **Chicago Tribune**
chicagotribune.com/

■ **Detroit News Direct**
detnews.com

■ **European Newspapers**
www.nyu.edu/pages/unionlist/

■ **Fox News**
www.foxnews.com

■ **InfoJunkie**
www.infojunkie.com/

■ **Los Angeles Times**
www.latimes.com/

■ **Morrock News Service**
www.morrock.com/

■ **MSNBC**
www.msnbc.com/news/default.asp

■ **Nando Times**
www.nando.net/

■ **NBC News**
www.nbc.com/

■ **New York Times**
www.nytimes.com/

■ **Newsies on the Web**
www.newsies.com/

■ **Newsroom**
www.auburn.edu/~vestmon/news.html

■ **NPR Online**
www.npr.org/

■ **Online NewsHour**
www.pbs.org/newshour/

■ **Point**
www.pbs.org/point/

■ **Positive Press**
www.positivepress.com/

■ **Real News Page**
www.rain.org/~openmind/realnews.htm

■ **Russia Today**
www.russiatoday.com/

■ **San Francisco Chronicle**
www.sfgate.com/chronicle/index.shtml

■ **San Francisco Examiner**
www.examiner.com/

■ **Sun-Sentinel**
www.sun-sentinel.com/

■ **Touch Today**
www.clickit.com/touch/news/news.htm

■ **TV News**
www.tfs.net/personal/gbyron/tvnews1.html

■ **U.S. News**
www.usnews.com/usnews/

■ **USA Today**
www.usatoday.com

■ **Washington Post**
www.washingtonpost.com/

■ **Yahoo News Image Gallery**
dailynews.yahoo.com/headlines/g/ts/

Nothing Better to Do

We don't claim that these sites have any value. We're talking soap operas and lost socks here. But if you truly have nothing better to do, take a quick look.

■ **An Entirely Other Day**
www.eod.com/index.html

■ **Anonymous Messenger**
www.smalltime.com/nowhere/anon/

■ **April Fools**
www.aprilfools.com

■ **As the Web Turns**
www.metzger.com/soap/

■ **Bad Cookie**
krug.org/badcookie/fortune.hts?badcookie

■ **Bizarre Stuff You Can Make in Your Kitchen**
freeweb.pdq.net/headstrong/

■ **Blank Page**
www.avnet.co.uk/russ-sky/blank.htm

■ **Boring Institute**
www.boringinstitute.com/

■ **Bureau of Missing Socks**
www.jagat.com/joel/socks.html

■ **Contest Catalogue**
contest.catalogue.com/contests/

■ **Cool404**
www.cool404.com

■ **Dancing Robot**
www.multimania.com/goprof/fsdancer.htm

■ **Distortions**
www.quirked.com/distortions/

■ **Electro Magnetic Poetry**
prominence.com/java/poetry/

■ **Elvis Lives**
wsrv.clas.virginia.edu/~acs5d/elvis.html

■ **Extra Crispy**
www.extracrispy.com/

■ **Famous Insults**
members.aol.com/WordPlays/insultfp.html

■ **Famous People's Wills**
www.ca-probate.com/wills.htm

■ **Flat Earth Society**
www.flat-earth.org/

■ **Flying Pigs**
user.icx.net/~midgard/favlinks/
favlinks.htm

■ **Futile**
www.futile.com/index2.html

■ **Gallery of Misused
Quotation Marks**
www.juvalamu.com/qmarks/

■ **Hair Police**
www.hairpolice.com/

■ **IQ Test**
www.iqtest.com/

■ **Klutz**
www.klutz.com/

■ **Mister Poll**
www.misterpoll.com/

■ **Most Annoying Sites**
www.annoyances.com/annoying.html

■ **Nostradamus Toolkit**
www.amae.com/

■ **Obsessive Fans**
countingdown.com/fans/

■ **Other People's Problems**
www2.paramount.com/opp/index.html

■ **Rhyme Generator**
www.pangloss.com/seidel/Poem/

■ **Rogue Market**
roguemarket.com/

■ **Rubberband Ball**
www.easttexas.com/pdlg/theball.htm

■ **Scary Sites of the Net**
people.ce.mediaone.net/bcbeatty/scary.htm

■ **The Ratings**
www.brunching.com/ratings/

■ **The Spot**
www.thespot.com

■ **This Is True**
www.thisistrue.com/

■ **Urban Legends Archive**
www.urbanlegends.com/

■ **Voyeur**
voyeur.mckinley.com/cgi-bin/voyeur.cgi

■ **Weeno**
www.weeno.com/

■ **Where's George?**
www.wheresgeorge.com/

■ **Yesterland**
www.mcs.net/~werner/yester.html

Online 'Zines—Internet and Computer

It's a natural: Use a computer forum to write about computers. The magazines here fall into two categories: those that are online versions of printed matter and those that stand on their own on the Internet.

■ **Byte**
www.byte.com/

■ **Computer Connections**
www.computerconnections.com/

■ **Computer News Daily**
www.computernewsdaily.com/

■ **ComputerWorld**
www.computerworld.com

■ **Dr. Dobbs Journal**
www.ddj.com/

■ **HotWired**
www.hotwired.com

■ **Hyperstand**
www.hyperstand.com/

■ **Interactive Week**
www4.zdnet.com/intweek/

■ **Internet World**
www.internetworld.com/

■ **Internet.com**
www.internet.com/

■ **Mac Today**
mactoday.com/

■ **Macworld**
macworld.zdnet.com/

■ **Media Central**
www.mediacentral.com/

■ **Netsurfer Digest**
www.netsurf.com/nsd/index.html

■ **NewsLinx**
www.newslinx.com/

■ **Next Generation**
www.next-generation.com/

■ **PC Computing**
www.zdnet.com/pccomp/

■ **PC Magazine**
www.pcmag.com/

■ **PC Today**
www.pctoday.com/

■ **Road Warrior News**
warrior.com/index.html

■ **Sip from the Firehose**
www.borland.com/firehose/

■ **Slate**
www.slate.com/

- **Smart Computing**
www.smartcomputing.com/Default.asp
- **Stating the Obvious**
www.theobvious.com/index.html
- **The Net Net**
www.thenetnet.com/
- **Web Magazine**
www.webmagazine.com/
- **Web Review**
www.webreview.com/
- **WebNovice Online**
www.webnovice.com/
- **Windows Magazine**
www.winmag.com/
- **Wired News**
www.wired.com/news/
- **Yahoo Internet Life**
www.yil.com

Online 'Zines—Varied

Other than information about the Internet itself, perhaps no type of site has grown as quickly as the online magazine. This selection demonstrates the diversity of the offerings.

- **American Newspeak**
www.scn.org/news/newspeak/

■ **Atlantic Monthly**
www.theatlantic.com

■ **Bad Golf**
www.badgolfmonthly.com/

■ **Billboard**
www.billboard-online.com/

■ **Black World Today**
www.tbwt.com/

■ **Captivated**
www.captivated.com/

■ **Cheapskate Monthly**
www.cheapsk8.com/

■ **Communication Arts**
www.commarts.com/

■ **Cricket Magazine Group**
www.cricketmag.com/home.html

■ **Daily Muse**
www.cais.net/aschnedr/muse.htm

■ **DesertUSA**
www.desertusa.com/

■ **Disgruntled**
www.disgruntled.com

■ **Farm Journal Today**
www.farmjournal.com

■ **Feed**
www.feedmag.com/

■ **Firehouse**
www.firehouse.com/

■ **Gadget**
www.gadgetnews.com/

■ **George**
www.georgemag.com

■ **Go Inside**
goinside.com/

■ **increase and diffusion**
www.si.edu/i+d/

■ **Inquisitor**
www.inquisitor.com/

■ **Journal X**
www.journalx.com/

■ **Literal Latte**
www.literal-latte.com/

■ **Lumiere**
www.lumiere.com/

■ **Metajournals**
www.metajournals.com/

■ **Mississippi Review**
sushi.st.usm.edu/mrw/

■ **National Geographic**
www.nationalgeographic.com/

■ **Officina Bohemia**
www.bohemialab.com/

■ **Old Farmer's Almanac**
www.almanac.com

■ **Oyster Boy Review**
sunsite.unc.edu/ob/index.html

■ **Papermag**
www.papermag.com/

■ **Personal Technology from the Wall Street Journal**
ptech.wsj.com/

■ **Retro**
www.retroactive.com/

■ **Roll Call**
www.rollcall.com/

■ **RollingStone**
www.rollingstone.com/

■ **Salon**
www.salonmagazine.com

■ **Scientific American**
www.sciam.com/

■ **Spaceviews**
www.spaceviews.com/

■ **Straight Dope**
www.straightdope.com/

■ **Supernation**
www.supernation.com/

■ **Surfer Mag**
www.surfermag.com/

■ **Technology Review**
www.techreview.com/

■ **Urban Desires**
www.desires.com/

■ **Utne Online**
www.utne.com/
■ **Vapor Trails**
www.vaportrails.com/
■ **Village Voice**
www.villagevoice.com/
■ **VolumeOne**
www.volumeone.com/
■ **Whole Pop**
www.wholepop.com/
■ **Y'all**
www.yall.com/
■ **ZineZone**
www.zinezone.com/

Outdoor Recreation

Resources and advice and places to go—it's all here.

■ **23 Peaks**
www.23peaks.com/
■ **ActiveUSA**
www.activeusa.com/
■ **All Outdoors**
www.alloutdoors.com/
■ **Appalachian Trail**
www.fred.net/kathy/at.html

■ **Backpacker**
www.thebackpacker.com/

■ **Big Wall Climbing**
www.primenet.com/~midds/

■ **Body Glove**
www.bodyglove.com/

■ **CampNet America**
www.kiz.com/campnet/html/campnet.htm

■ **Divernet**
www.divernet.com/

■ **E-Flight**
e-flight.com/e-flight/

■ **Everest Online**
www.everestonline.com/

■ **FishingWorld**
www.fishingworld.com/Entry.html

■ **Global Oceanic Surfing**
magna.com.au/~prfbrown/tubelink.html

■ **Global Orienteering Links**
www.shef.ac.uk/uni/union/susoc/suoc/
links.html

■ **Go Camping America**
www.gocampingamerica.com

■ **Grand Tour**
www.princeton.edu/~oa/oa.html

■ **Great Outdoor Recreational Page**
www.gorp.com

■ **GreatOutdoors**
greatoutdoors.com/

■ **Hiking and Walking**
www.teleport.com/~walking/hiking.html

■ **Horse Trails**
www.horsetrails.com/

■ **Mad About Mountains**
www.personal.u-net.com/~keswick/home.htm

■ **Mountain Bike Resources**
www.mbronline.com/

■ **Mountain Zone**
www.mountainzone.com/toc.html

■ **National Caves**
www.cavern.com/

■ **National Park Service**
www.nps.gov/

■ **Outdoor Action**
www.princeton.edu/~oa/oa.html

■ **Outdoor Adventure Sports**
www.outdoorsource.com/

■ **Outdoor Explorer**
http://www.outdoorexplorer.com/

■ **Outdoor Resource**
www.outdoorsource.com/

■ **Outside Online**
outside.starwave.com/

■ **Outward Bound**
www.outwardbound.org/intro-01.html

■ **Park Search**
www.llbean.com/parksearch/

■ **Parks Around the World**
www.gorp.com/gorp/resource/
US_National_Park/intlpark.htm

■ **Pilots and Aviation**
www.landings.com/aviation.html

■ **Quokka**
www.quokka.com/

■ **Red River Diary**
www.manflood.com/

■ **Rock and Ice**
www.rockandice.com/

■ **State Parks Online**
www.mindspring.com/~wxrnot/parks.html

■ **TrailWalk**
www.trailwalk.com/

■ **Volksmarch Index**
www.ava.org/

■ **Waterparks**
www.waterparks.com/

■ **WinterNet**
www.iion.com/WinterNet/index.html

People Connection

If you want to find someone you know or find out something about someone you don't know, Internet resources outstrip all others.

- **Bigfoot**
www.bigfoot.com/
- **Celebrity Chronicle**
www.polaris.net/~merlin/fame.html
- **Child Quest**
www.childquest.org/
- **ClassMates Online**
www.classmates.com/
- **Directory of High School Reunions**
www.memorysite.com/reunions/
- **Faces of Adoption**
www.inet.net/adopt/
- **GTE SuperPages**
superpages.gte.net/
- **I Knew Them When**
www.iknewthemwhen.com/
- **Liszt**
www.liszt.com/
- **Missing Persons**
missing.inthe.net/index.asp
- **Notable Citizens of Planet Earth**
www.search.com/Single/0,7,200482,00.html
- **Personal Pages Worldwide**
www.utexas.edu/world/personal/index.html
- **PlanetAll**
www.planetall.com
- **Real People, Real Stories**
members.aol.com/gmanacsa/realpage.html

- **Reunion Hall**
www.xscom.com/reunion/
- **ReunionNet**
www.reunited.com/
- **Seeker**
www.the-seeker.com/
- **Six Degrees of Separation**
www.sixdegrees.com/
- **Student.com**
www.student.com/feature/ppd/
- **Switchboard**
www.switchboard.com/
- **Ultimate People Finder**
www.knowx.com/free/peoplefinder.htm
- **Webgrrls**
www.webgrrls.com/
- **WhoWhere**
www.whowhere.com/

Performing Arts

Opera, ballet, mime, and other activities that involve performances can be found here.

- **American Ballet Theater**
www.abt.org/
- **ArtsEdge**
artsedge.kennedy-center.org/

■ **ArtsLynx**
www.artslynx.org/

■ **Ballet Dictionary**
www.abt.org/dictionary/

■ **Bolshoi Theater**
www.bolshoi.ru/eng/frame.html

■ **Carnegie Hall**
www.carnegiehall.org/

■ **Coleman Theatre**
www.coleman.miami.ok.us/

■ **CultureFinder**
www.culturefinder.com/index.htm

■ **Culturekiosque**
www.culturekiosque.com/

■ **Cyberdance**
www.thepoint.net/~raw/dance.htm

■ **European Network of the Performing Arts**
www.ecna.org/enicpa/

■ **International Society for the Performing Arts Foundation**
ispa-online.org/

■ **John F. Kennedy Center for the Performing Arts**
www.kennedy-center.org/

■ **Le Centre du Silence**
www.indranet.com/lcds.html

■ **Opera America**
www.operaam.org/

■ **Opera Schedule Server**
www.fsz.bme.hu/opera/main.html

■ **Performing Arts Data Services**
www.pads.ahds.ac.uk/

■ **Performing Arts Studio**
www.pastudio.com/

■ **Royal Opera House**
www.royalopera.org/

■ **Royal Shakespeare Company**
www.rsc.org.uk/

■ **San Francisco Opera**
www.sfopera.com/

■ **Stomp**
www.stomponline.com/

■ **Voice of Dance**
www.voiceofdance.org/Dance/

Photography

Both professional and amateur samples are available for your viewing pleasure and, possibly, purchase.

■ **Black Star**
www.blackstar.com/

■ **California Museum of Photography**
cmpl.ucr.edu

■ **Cheese Magazine**
www.cheesemagazine.com/

■ **Clique**
www.clique.org/

■ **Converge**
idt.net/~robertp/

■ **Corbis**
www.corbis.com

■ **Images of Jazz**
www.leonardjazz.com/

■ **Index Stock**
www.indexstock.com

■ **Lightbox**
www.netlink.co.uk/users/lightbox/

■ **Masters of Photography**
masters-of-photography.com/

■ **Mountain Gallery**
www.cs.berkeley.edu/~qtluong/gallery/

■ **Mythopoeia**
www.myth.com/

■ **PhotoDisc**
www.photodisc.com/

■ **Spy-cams**
www.spy-cams.com/

■ **StockPhoto**
www.s2f.com/STOCKPHOTO/

■ **Stock Solution**
www.tssphoto.com

■ **Storm Photos**
www.photolib.noaa.gov/

■ **The Sight3**
thesight.com/

■ **Times Square Photography Project**
www.timessquarephotos.org/

■ **Underwater Photography**
www.ozemail.com.au/~billwood/

■ **ZoneZero**
www.zonezero.com/

■ **White House News
Photographers Association**
www.whnpa.org/

Political Science

If you are interested in a specific political issue, be assured that a search engine will locate many sites on that topic. The sites listed here, however, are generic and address the overall political scene.

■ **AllPolitics**
AllPolitics.com/

■ **America Votes**
scriptorium.lib.duke.edu/americavotes/

■ **Campaigns and Elections**
www.camelect.com/

■ **Candidates, Campaigns,
and Elections**
www.votenet.com/

■ **Capitol Hill Blue**
www.capitolhillblue.com/index.htm

■ **CitizenDirect**
www.citizendirect.net/

■ **Congressional Q & A**
www.c-span.org/questions/

■ **Digital Democracy**
www.cdt.org/action/

■ **Do It Yourself
Congressional Investigation**
www.crp.org/diykit/

■ **Election Connection**
www.gspm.org/electcon/

■ **Election Notes**
www.klipsan.com/elecnews.htm

■ **Elections Around the World**
www.agora.stm.it/elections/election/
home.htm

■ **Federal Election Commission**
www.fec.gov/

■ **Gallup Organization**
www.gallup.com/

■ **In the Public Interest**
www.sfbg.com/nader/

■ **Jefferson Project**
www.capweb.net/classic/jefferson/

■ **National Election Studies**
www.umich.edu/~nes/

■ **National Political Index**
www.politicalindex.com/

■ **Net Vote**
netvote98.mci.com/register.html

■ **Open Secrets**
www.opensecrets.org/home/index.asp

■ **Opinion Polls**
www.pollingreport.com/

■ **Policy.com**
www.policy.com/

■ **Political Database of the Americas**
www.georgetown.edu/pdba/

■ **Political Graveyard**
www.potifos.com/tpg/

■ **Political Site of the Day**
www.aboutpolitics.com/

■ **Politics1**
www.politics1.com/

■ **PollingReport**
www.pollingreport.com/

■ **Public Campaign**
www.publicampaign.org/

■ **Public Citizen**
www.citizen.org/

■ **Publics Affairs Web**
www.publicaffairsweb.com/

■ **Roll Call**
www.rollcall.com/

■ **Soft Money Laundromat**
www.commoncause.org/laundromat/

■ **The Hill**
www.hillnews.com/

■ **Third Party Time?**
www.ksg.harvard.edu/case/3pt/

■ **Web White and Blue**
www.webwhiteblue.org/

■ **White House Project**
www.thewhitehouseproject.org/index2.html

Reference and Research

A key advantage of the Internet is that you can find information about just about anything. These particular sites specialize in organizing some of that information and presenting it in a searchable manner.

■ **10,000 Year Calendar**
calendarhome.com/tyc/

■ **50 State Capitals**
www.flags.net/

■ **Acronym Lookup**
www.ucc.ie/cgi-bin/acronym

■ **Acronyms and Abbreviations**
www.ucc.ie/cgi-bin/acronym

■ **Annals of Improbable Research**
www.improb.com/

■ **Ask Dr. Dictionary**
www.dictionary.com/

■ **Bartlett's Familiar Quotations**
www.cc.columbia.edu/acis/bartleby/bartlett/

■ **Best Information on the Net**
www.hitline.ch/ger/homepage/jacob/
gratis.htm

■ **Biographical Dictionary**
www-groups.dcs.st-
andrews.ac.uk/%7Ehistory/
Alphabetical.html

■ **Britannica Online**
www.eb.com

■ **CIA World Factbook**
www.odci.gov/cia/publications/factbook/
index.html

■ **Common Errors in English**
www.wsu.edu:8080/~brians/errors/
index.html

■ **Copyright Archive**
copyrightarchive.com

■ **Encyclopedia of Mythology**
www.pins.co.uk/upages/probertm/
myths.htm

■ **FAQs by Category**
www.lib.ox.ac.uk/internet/news/faq/
by_category.index.html

■ **Federal Web Locator**
www.law.vill.edu/fed-agency/fedwebloc.html

■ **Flags of All Countries**
www.wave.net/upg/immigration/flags.html

■ **Funk and Wagnalls Encyclopedia**
www.funkandwagnalls.com/

■ **Guinness Book of Records**
www.guinnessrecords.com/

■ **Harper's Index**
www.harpers.org/harpers-index/
harpers-index.html

■ **Index of Biographies**
www-groups.dcs.st-andrews.ac.uk/
%7Ehistory/Alphabetical.html

■ **Information Please**
www.infoplease.com/

■ **Library of Congress Reading Room**
lcweb.loc.gov/global/ncp/ncp.html

■ **Library Spot**
www.libraryspot.com/

■ **Measurement Converter**
www.mplik.ru:8081/~sg/transl/

■ **National Archives**
www.nara.gov/

■ **Nobel Channel**
www.nobelchannel.com/nsapi/index.html

▲ www.nobelchannel.com/nsapi/index.html

■ **Office of Population Research**
opr.princeton.edu/

■ **Online Intelligence Project**
www.icg.org/intelweb/index.html

■ **Online Reference Works**
www.cs.cmu.edu/references.html

■ **Plumb Design's Thesaurus**
www.plumbdesign.com/thesaurus

■ **Police Ten Codes**
www.provide.net/~bfield/10codes.html

■ **Pop Clocks**
www.census.gov/main/www/popclock.html

■ **Ready Reference Collection**
www.ipl.org/ref/RR/

■ **Researchpaper.com**
www.researchpaper.com/index.html

■ **Roget's Thesaurus**
www.thesaurus.com/

■ **Southwest Research Institute**
www.swri.org/

■ **Thomas: Legislative Information**
thomas.loc.gov

■ **United States Code**
uscode.house.gov/usc.htm

■ **Virtual Reference Desk**
thorplus.lib.purdue.edu/reference/

■ **World Flags**
www.flags.net/

- **World Time**
www.worldtime.com/
- **Yellow Pages USA**
www.bigyellow.com/

Resume Services

Most of these folks will post your web page resume on their site, sometimes free, but usually for a fee. Some also offer advice on making resumes. Others offer resume services as just one service of many.

- **#1 Resume Writing Services**
www.free-resume-tips.com/
- **10 Minute Resume**
www.10minuteresume.com/
- **1st Impressions Resumes**
www.1st-imp.com/
- **A+ Online Resumes**
www.ol-resume.com/
- **Aicron Resume Services**
www.aicron.com/
- **Career Shop**
www.careershop.com/
- **Career Site**
www.careersite.com/
- **Eagle's Resume Services**
www.richmwww.aicron.com/ond.infi.net/
~leeann/

■ **Guaranteed Resume**
www.gresumes.com/

■ **How to Write a Resume**
www.trincoll.edu/admin/career/
how_to_guides/resume.shtml

■ **JobDirect**
www.jobdirect.com/

■ **Resume Design**
www.ssd.sscc.ru/misc/Resume/

■ **Resume Innovations**
www.resume-innovations.com/

■ **Resume Publishing Company**
www.sni.net/cha/trpc.htm

■ **Resume Store**
www.resumestore.com/main.html

■ **Resume White Papers**
www.goodnet.com/~bf90682/rwp/

■ **Resume World**
www.resunet.com/rw/

■ **ResumeNet**
www.resumenet.com/

■ **Resumes on the Web**
www.resweb.com/

■ **Sample Dynamic Cover Letters**
www.stetson.edu/~rhansen/covexam.html

■ **Technical Resume Writing Tips**
www.taos.com/resumetips.html

■ **Tripod's Resume Builder**
www.tripod.com/explore/jobs_career/
resume/

■ **Virtual Resume**
www.virtualresume.com/

■ **Writing a Persuasive Cover Letter**
www.golden.net/~archeus/covlet1.htm

Robotics

Most sites reflect current robotics developments in university or government labs. But some are commercial or personal sites.

■ **Basic BEAM Robotics**
members.xoom.com/robots/index.htm

■ **Berkeley Robotics Lab**
robotics.eecs.berkeley.edu/

■ **Cambridge Speech Vision and Robotics**
svr-www.eng.cam.ac.uk/

■ **Cool Robot of the Week**
ranier.hq.nasa.gov/telerobotics_page/
coolrobots.html

■ **Harvard Robotics Laboratory**
hrl.harvard.edu/

■ **Lab for Perceptual Robotics**
www-robotics.cs.umass.edu/lpr.html

■ **Laboratory for Perceptual Robotics**
piglet.cs.umass.edu

■ **Laboratory Robotics Interest Group**
lab-robotics.org/

■ **Mobile Robot Laboratory**
www.cc.gatech.edu/aimosaic/
robot-lab/MRLHome.html

■ **NASA Space Telerobotics Programs**
ranier.hq.nasa.gov/telerobotics_page/
telerobotics.shtm

■ **NASA Space Telerobotics**
ranier.oact.hq.nasa.gov/telerobotics.html

■ **Real World Interface**
falcon.rwii.com/

■ **RoboShopper**
www.roboshopper.com/

■ **Robot Home Page**
www.areacom.it/html/arte_cultura/
warworld/ROBOT.HTM

■ **Robot Wars**
ranier.hq.nasa.gov/telerobotics_page/
coolrobots.html

■ **Robotics FAQs**
www.frc.ri.cmu.edu/robotics-faq/

■ **Robotics Research**
www.cs.man.ac.uk/robotics/

■ **Robotics Resources**
www.eg.bucknell.edu/~robotics/
res_frame.html

■ **Stanford Robotics Lab**
robotics.stanford.edu/

Save the People

If you want to help, or want to be helped, these sites offer plenty of information about getting started.

■ **54 Ways You Can Help the Homeless**
www.earthsystems.org/ways/

■ **Amnesty International**
www.amnesty.org/

■ **Charitable Choices**
www.charitablechoices.org/

■ **CharityNet**
www.idealist.org/

■ **Disaster Relief**
www.disasterrelief.org/

■ **Habitat for Humanity**
www.habitat.org/

■ **HungerWeb**
www.brown.edu/Departments/
World_Hunger_Program/

■ **I Have a Dream Foundation**
www.ihad.org/

- **Idealist**
www.idealist.org/
- **Impact Online**
www.webcom.com/~iol/
- **InterAction**
www.interaction.org/
- **Internet Nonprofit Center**
www.nonprofits.org/
- **National Coalition for the Homeless**
nch.ari.net/
- **Peace Corps**
www.peacecorps.gov/home.html
- **Salvation Army**
www.salvationarmyusa.org/home.htm
- **Second Harvest**
www.secondharvest.org/
- **UNICEF**
www.unicef.org/
- **U.S. Committee for Refugees**
www.refugees.org/

Save the Planet

As you can see, many people are already involved in organizations to help the environment. You can check out what they are doing, perhaps take some of their tips for everyday living, or even join them.

Save the Planet

■ **6 Billion Human Beings**
www.popexpo.net/english.html

■ **American Forests**
www.amfor.org/

■ **Arbor Day**
www.arborday.com/

■ **Bagheera**
www.bagheera.com/

■ **Climate Action Network**
www.climatenetwork.org/

■ **Compost Resource Page**
www.oldgrowth.org/compost/

■ **Conservation International**
www.conservation.org/

■ **Corporate Watch**
www.corpwatch.org/

■ **Dolphins: Oracles of the Sea**
library.advanced.org/17963/

■ **Eagle Page**
www.sky.net/~emily/eagle.html

■ **Earth Share**
www.earthshare.org/

■ **EnviroLink**
www.envirolink.org/

■ **Environmental Legislation**
www.nrdc.org/nrdc/field/state.html

■ **Environmental Stresses and Tree Health**
www.ianr.unl.edu/pubs/forestry/G1036.htm

■ **Environmental Yellow Pages**
www.enviroyellowpages.com/

■ **Forests Forever**
www.forestsforever.org/

■ **Friends of the Earth**
www.foe.co.uk/

■ **Friends of the Environment**
www.fef.ca/

■ **Garbage**
www.learner.org/exhibits/garbage/intro.html

■ **Global Eco-Village**
www.gaia.org/

■ **Green Lane**
www.doe.ca/envhome.html

■ **GreenMoney Online**
www.greenmoney.com/

■ **Greenpeace**
www.greenpeaceusa.org/

■ **Greenways**
www2.greenways.com/greenways/

■ **International Rivers Network**
www.irn.org/

- **Living Africa**
hyperion.advanced.org/16645/
contents.html
- **Nature Conservancy**
www.tnc.org/
- **Planet Ark**
www.planetark.org/
- **Rainforest Action Network**
www.ran.org/ran/
- **Recycler's World**
www.recycle.net/recycle/index.html
- **Rotten Truth About Garbage**
www.astc.org/info/exhibits/rotten/
rthome.htm
- **Save the Beaches**
beaches.hartford.edu/
- **Sea Turtle Survival**
www.cccturtle.org/
- **Search Your Watershed**
www.epa.gov/surf2/surf98/wimdw.html
- **Seaweb**
www.seaweb.org/
- **Sierra Club**
www.sierraclub.org/
- **Silicon Valley Joint Venture**
www.jointventure.org/
- **Solstice**
solstice.crest.org/index.shtml

■ **Turtle Trax**
www.turtles.org/

■ **Whole Earth**
www.wholeearthmag.com/

■ **Wildlife Web**
www.selu.com/~bio/wildlife/

■ **Wilerness Society**
wilderness.org/

■ **Wolf's Den**
www.wolfsden.org/

■ **World Conservation**
www.wcmc.org.uk/

■ **World Map for Whale Watchers**
www.physics.helsinki.fi/whale/world.html

■ **World Wildlife Federation**
www.wwf.org/

Science

Scientific interests have been presented on the Internet from the beginning. If you are involved in science in any way, whether you are merely taking a class or make your living in the scientific community or simply have a keen curiosity, your particular interest is probably represented in several sites on the Internet. See also Mathematics.

■ **Amusement Park Physics**
www.learner.org/exhibits/parkphysics/

Science

■ **Ask the Astronomer**
www2.ari.net/home/odenwald/qadir/
qanda.html

■ **Bad Science Page**
www.ems.psu.edu/~fraser/BadScience.html

■ **Biographies of Scientists**
www.blupete.com/Literature/Biographies/
Science/Scients.htm

■ **Biology Project**
www.biology.arizona.edu/

■ **BioTech**
biotech.icmb.utexas.edu/

■ **Botanical Glossaries**
sln.fi.edu/biosci/heart.html

■ **ChemFinder**
chemfinder.camsoft.com/

■ **Community of Science**
www.cos.com/

■ **Cool Science Images**
whyfiles.news.wisc.edu/coolimages/

■ **Dinosauria Online**
www.dinosauria.com/

■ **Explore Science**
www.explorescience.com/

■ **FIRST**
www.usfirst.org/

■ **FlyBase**
flybase.bio.indiana.edu

■ **Galileo's Notes on Motion**
www.imss.fi.it/ms72/

■ **General Chemistry**
chemfinder.camsoft.com/

■ **History of Science and Technology**
www.asap.unimelb.edu.au/hstm/
hstm_ove.htm

■ **How Things Work**
landau1.phys.virginia.edu/Education/
Teaching/HowThingsWork/home.html

■ **Human Anatomy Online**
www.innerbody.com/

■ **Human Brain**
uta.marymt.edu/~psychol/brain.html

■ **Last Word**
www.last-word.com/

■ **Newton's Apple**
ericir.syr.edu/Projects/Newton/

■ **Nobel Foundation**
www.nobel.se/

■ **Ozone Hole Tour**
www.atm.ch.cam.ac.uk/tour/

■ **Physics FAQ**
math.ucr.edu/home/baez/physics/faq.html

■ **Profiles in Science**
www.profiles.nlm.nih.gov/

■ **Quantum Computation**
www.qubit.org/

■ **Science a GoGo**
www.scienceagogo.com/

■ **Science Daily**
www.sciencedaily.com/

■ **Science in the Public Interest**
www.cspinet.org/

■ **Science Odyssy**
www.pbs.org/wgbh/aso/

■ **Science Whatzit**
www.omsi.edu/online/whatzit/home.html

■ **Scientific American**
www.sciam.com/

■ **Split-Cycle Engine**
www.ozemail.aust.com/~splitcyc/

■ **The Heart**
sln.fi.edu/biosci/heart.html

■ **The Why Files**
whyfiles.news.wisc.edu/

■ **Transistor Science**
www.pbs.org/transistor/

■ **Virtual Frog Dissection Kit**
george.lbl.gov/ITG.hm.pg.docs/dissect/
info.html

■ **Visible Human Viewer**
www.npac.syr.edu/projects/vishuman/
VisibleHuman.html

■ **Visible Human**
www.nlm.nih.gov/research/visible/
visible_human.html

■ **Volcano World**
volcano.und.nodak.edu/vw.html

Shopping—Books

If you want a particular book that is old, rare, or a bestseller, it's on the Internet. If you just want to browse, the choices are wonderfully endless.

■ **Alternative Books Superstore**
web-star.com/alternative/books.html

■ **Amazon Books**
www.amazon.com

■ **AnyBook International**
www.anybook.com/

■ **Bargain Book Warehouse**
www.1bookstreet.com/1bargainbookstreet/
Bargain_Home.asp

■ **Barnes and Noble**
www.barnesandnoble.com/

■ **Boat Books**
www.webworkshop.com/boatbooks/

■ **Book Collectors Bookstore**
www.abcbooks.com/

■ **Book Passage**
www.bookpassage.com/

■ **Bookpool Technical Books**
www.bookpool.com/

■ **Books.com**
www.books.com

■ **Borders**
www.borders.com/

■ **Clean Well-lighted Place for Books**
www.bookstore.com/

■ **Computer and Internet books**
hoganbooks.com/freebook/webbooks.html

■ **Fatbrain**
www.clbooks.com/

■ **Libros en Espanol**
www.sbdbooks.com/

■ **Midnight Special Bookstore**
www2.msbooks.com/msbooks/
homepage.html

■ **Serendipity Books**
www.serendipitybooks.com/

■ **Varsity Books**
www.varsitybooks.com/

■ **Vintage Bookstore**
www.vintagelibrary.com/index.cfm

■ **Virtual Moe's**
moesbooks.com/

■ **Wantagh Rare Book Company**
www.zelacom.com/~wantagh/

Shopping—Catalogs

Order from the catalog or order from the Internet.

■ **Bloomingdale's**
www.bloomingdales.com/

■ **Books on Tape**
www.booksontape.com/

■ **CatalogLink**
cataloglink.com/cl/

■ **Disney Store**
disney.go.com/Shopping/

■ **Eastbay**
www.eastbay.com/

■ **Eddie Bauer**
www.ebauer.com/

■ **Harry and David**
www.harryanddavid.com/

■ **Jackson and Perkins**
www.jacksonandperkins.com/

■ **JCPenney**
www.jcpenney.com/shopping

■ **L. L. Bean**
www.llbean.com/

■ **Lands' End**
www.landsend.com/

■ **Neiman Marcus**
www.neimanmarcus.com/

■ **Popcorn Factory**
www.thepopcornfactory.com/

■ **REI**
www.rei.com/

■ **Spiegel**
www.spiegel.com/spiegel

■ **Talbots**
www.talbots.com/

■ **The Company Store**
www.thecompanystore.com/

■ **The Nature Company**
www.natureco.com/

■ **Watkins Product Catalog**
futuregate.com/watkins_catalog/index.html

Shopping—Classifieds

These Internet ads resemble the classifieds ads in newspapers. All sites here are easy to search.

■ **#1 Classifieds**
www.boconline.com/1Classifieds/1fieds.htm

■ **4* Classifieds**
www.4starads.com/classifieds/

■ **AdQuest**
www.adquest3d.com/

■ **American Internet Classifieds**
www.bestads.com/

■ **Buy and Sell**
www.buy-and-sell.com/

■ **Classified Display**
www.classified-display.com/

■ **Classified Warehouse**
www.classifiedwarehouse.com/index.html

- **ClassiFIND**
www.classifind.com/

- **Classify It**
www.classify-it.com/

- **EMarket Trading Post**
www.emrkt.com/trading_post/

- **Epage Internet Classifieds**
www.ep.com/

- **Free Classified Ads**
www.freeclassifiedads.com/

- **LookSmart Classifieds**
www.classifieds2000.com/cgi-cls/
display.exe?looksmart+class

- **Swap and Shop**
swapandshop.com/club.htm

- **The Find**
www.thefind.com/default_tf.asp

- **Trader Online Classified Ads**
www.traderonline.com/

Shopping—Computer Hardware, Software, and Stuff

Serious computerphiles can spend many hours sorting out the wares offered by these sites.

- **Baber's Global Computer Directory**
www.baber.com/

■ **Best Buy**
www.bestbuy.com/

■ **Beyond.com**
www.beyond.com/

■ **Black Box**
www.blackbox.com/

■ **Build Your Own PC**
www.verinet.com/pc/

■ **BuyDirect**
www.buydirect.com/?st.snap.dir

■ **Compubooks**
www.compubooks.com/

■ **CompUSA Online**
www.compusa.com

■ **Computer Craft**
www.ccraft.net

■ **Computer Discount Warehouse**
www.cdw.com/

■ **Computer Quick**
www.cqk.com/

■ **Computer Shopper**
www5.zdnet.com/cshopper/

■ **Cybercalifragilistic**
www.webcom.com/getagift/

■ **Cybermedia**
www.cybermedia.com/

■ **Download.com**
www.download.com/

■ **Egghead Software**
www.egghead.com/

■ **ElectronicsNet**
www.electronics.net/

■ **E-Town**
www.e-town.com/

■ **Exploria**
www.exploria.com

■ **It's Time**
www2.viaweb.com/rks/itstim.html

■ **NECX Direct**
www.necx.com/

■ **Online Used Computer Swap**
www.creativelement.com/swap/

■ **Outpost.com**
web3.ops.outpost.com/

■ **PC Magazine Software**
www.zdnet.com/pcmag/pclabs/software/
software.htm

■ **PC Shopping Planet**
www.shoppingplanet.com/

■ **Price Watch**
www.pricewatch.com/

■ **Screen Savers Bonanza**
www.bonanzas.com/ssavers/index.html

■ **Second Nature Software**
www.secondnature.com/

- **Softchoice**
www.softchoice.com/

- **System Optimization**
www.sysopt.com/

- **TechShopper**
www.techweb.com/shopper/

- **TechWeb**
www.techweb.com/

- **Tom's Hardware Guide**
www.sysdoc.pair.com/

- **Ultimate Conversation Piece**
www.pe.net/~spcltees/

- **Zing**
www.zing.com

Shopping—General

Popular Internet shopping sites have been arbitrarily divided here into various categories. The "general" sites listed here tend to offer a variety of products or shopping-related services.

- **Acquired Taste**
www.acquiredtaste.com/

- **Alloy Online**
www.alloyonline.com/

- **Amish Country Network**
www.amishcountrynetwork.com/

■ **As Seen on TV**
www.asontv.com/

■ **At Your Office**
www.atyouroffice.com/

■ **Beyond Average Gear**
www.bagear.com/

■ **Bluefly**
www.bluefly.com/

■ **Buccaneer Trading Company**
www.buccaneer.net/

■ **Bugle Boy**
www.bugleboy.com/

■ **Bushel of Baskets**
www.abushelofbaskets.com/

■ **CDnow**
www.cdnow.com

■ **CD Universe**
www.cduniverse.com

■ **CompareNet**
www.compare.net/

■ **Cool Savings**
www.coolsavings.com

■ **Corral West Ranchwear**
www.corralwest.com/

■ **Coupon Clippers**
www.couponclippers.com/
signup_advertiser.htm

■ **CyberShop**
www.cybershop.com/

■ **Designer Deals**
www.designerdeals.com/

■ **Discount Games**
www.discountgames.com/

■ **Fashion Planet**
www.fashion-planet.com

■ **Filene's Basement**
www.filenesbasement.com/

■ **First Sightings**
www.firstsightings.com/

■ **Furniture.com**
www.furniture.com/

■ **Gap**
www.gap.com/onlinestore/gap/

■ **Gift Tree**
www.gifttree.com/

■ **Good Guys**
www.thegoodguys.com/frame_home.html

■ **IQVC**
www.iqvc.com

■ **MelaNet**
www.melanet.com/

■ **Music Boulevard**
www.musicblvd.com/

■ **mySimon**
www.mysimon.com/

- **NY Shopper**
www.bestnyonline.com/

- **Pacific Trekking**
pacifictrekking.com/

- **Patagonia**
www.patagonia.com/

- **Peapod**
www.peapod.com/

- **Quick Coupons**
www.qpons.com/

- **ReviewBooth**
www.reviewbooth.com/

- **Roxy**
www.roxy.com/

- **Sample Sale**
www.samplesale.com/

- **Sharper Image**
www.sharperimage.com/

- **Store4Kids**
www.store4kids.com/

- **Surplus/Closeout Finder**
www.infomart.net/surplus/

- **Tower Records**
www.tower.records

- **Toys 'R' Us**
www.toysrus.com/

- **Urbanwhere**
www.urbanwhere.com/

■ **Value America**
www.valueamerica.com/

■ **ValuPage**
www.valupage.com/

■ **Virtual Emporium**
www.virtualemporium.com/

■ **Wellspring Media**
www.wellmedia.com/

Shopping—Mall

Each site on this list is a collection of online stores, that is, it's the same idea as a bricks and mortar mall.

■ **Access Market Square**
www.amsquare.com/

■ **America Shopping Mall**
www.asmall.com/

■ **Awesome Mall**
malls.com/awesome/

■ **Big Planet**
www.bpstore.com/index.html

■ **Biggest Mall**
www.biggestmall.com/

■ **Choice Mall**
mall.choicemall.com/

■ **Coolshopping**
www.coolshopping.com/

■ **Cowboy Mall**
www.cowboymall.com/

■ **Downtown Anywhere**
www.awa.com/index.html

■ **Duluth Mall**
www.duluthemall.com/

■ **EcoMall**
www.ecomall.com/

■ **Empire Mall**
empiremall.com/

■ **Globalscape Mall**
www.sigmaduke.com/business/

■ **Great Alaskan Mall**
alaskan.com/

■ **Hall of Malls**
www.nsns.com/MouseTracks/hall/
general.html

■ **iMall**
www.imall.com/

■ **Mall of Cyberspace**
www.zmall.com/

■ **Mallpark**
www.mallpark.com/

■ **MarketSuite**
www.1ms.com/

■ **NeedleArts Mall**
www.needlearts.com/shop_index.html

■ **Pennsylvania Dutch Marketplace**
www.padutch.com/Welcome.html

■ **Point and Shop Mall**
www.fashionclub.org/

■ **Sell 'em**
www.sellem.com

■ **Shoparoo**
www.shoparoo.com/

■ **ShopNow**
www.shopnow.com/

■ **Shop-the-Malls**
www.shop-the-malls.com/toc.htm

■ **SkyMall**
www.skymall.com/

■ **Student Mall**
studentcenter.infomall.org/ourmall.html

■ **Supermall Association**
www.supermall-association.com/

■ **Texas Hill Country Mall**
www.texashillcountrymall.com/

■ **Tropical Mall**
www.naples-fl.com/

■ **Truly Texan**
www.trulytexan.com/

■ **USA Supermall**
www.usasupermall.com/

■ **Wild West Cybermall**
www.cache.net/westmall/

■ **World Wide Mall**
www.olworld.com/olworld/mall/mall_us/
dir.html

■ **WorldShop**
www.worldshop.com/

Shopping—Specialty

The sites in this list offer some specific product or product line—or are just cute little "shops."

■ **1001 Herbs**
www.1001herbs.com/

■ **1-800-Batteries**
www.1800batteries.com/home.htm

■ **1-800-Flowers**
www.1800flowers.com

■ **Aardvark Pet**
www.aardvarkpet.com/

■ **All About First Names**
www.personalizedgiftshop.com/

■ **American Quilts**
www.americanquilts.com/

■ **American Science and Surplus**
www.sciplus.com/

■ **Anything Left-handed**
members.aol.com/alhleft/

- **Archie McPhee**
www.mcphee.com/
- **Aspen Trading Post**
www.aspentradingpost.com/
- **Audio Highway**
www.audiohwy.com
- **Australian Wool Gallery**
www.exton.com/awg/
- **Azazz**
www.azazz.com/
- **BabyCenter Shopping**
www.babycenter.com/shopping/
- **Bird Houses**
www.carpenterslace.com/
- **Bliss Spa**
www.blissspa.com/
- **Brits Abroad**
www.britsabroad.co.uk/
- **Candy Direct**
www.candydirect.com/
- **Candlexpress**
www.candlexpress.com/
- **Cape Athletic**
www.capeathletic.com/
- **CBS Store**
marketing.cbs.com/store/
- **Charm Cheese**
www.craftassoc.com/charmcm.html

■ **Civil War Outpost**
www.civilwaroutpost.com/

■ **Clown Shoes**
www.jollywalkers.com/

■ **College Depot**
collegedepot.com/

■ **CrackerWhacker**
www.crackerwhacker.com/

■ **Curiosity Shoppe**
www.jstudios.com/curiosity/popup.htm

■ **Custom Pens and Pencils**
www.southwind.net/market/woodpens/

■ **DaFridge Magnets**
www.dafridge.com/

■ **Designer Stencils**
www.designerstencils.com/

■ **Down to Earth**
www.downtoearth.com/

■ **Fabric8**
www.fabric8.com/

■ **Farmacopia**
www.candydirect.com/

■ **Faucet Factory**
www.faucetfactory.com/

■ **Fogdog Sports**
www.fogdog.com/

■ **Fossil Company**
www.fossil-company.com/

■ **Fragrance Counter**
www.fragrancecounter.com/

■ **Gargoyle Statuary**
www.gargoylestatuary.com/

■ **Hammocks**
www.hameck.com/

■ **Hollywood Posters**
www.hollywoodsouvenirs.com/pms.html

■ **Hot Hot Hot**
www.hothothot.com

■ **Internet Antique Shop**
www.tias.com/

■ **Internet Bookshop**
www.bookshop.co.uk/

■ **Intima Watches**
www.intima.com/

■ **Jam, Jelly, and More**
www.vipimage.com/

■ **Joy of Socks**
www.joyofsocks.com/

■ **Justballs**
www.justballs.com/

■ **Kennedy Space Center Shop**
www.thespaceshop.com/

■ **Kite Store**
www.kitestore.com/kite/index.htm

■ **Louisana French Market**
www.louisianafrenchmarket.com/

■ **Maui Buy the Inch**
aloha-mall.com/buy-maui/

■ **Mexican Pottery**
www.awa.com/tp/

■ **Moon Spirit Gallery**
www.moonchild.com/moonspirit/

■ **Mother Nature's General Store**
www.mothernature.com/

■ **Mountain Zone**
www.mountainzone.com/

■ **Mrs. Fields Cookies**
www.mrsfields.com/

■ **Navajo Rugs**
navajorugs.spma.org/

■ **Perfect Present Picker**
presentpicker.com/

■ **Prima Sports**
www.prima.com/

■ **Red Rocket**
www.redrocket.com/

▲ www.redrocket.com

■ **Reel**
www.reel.com

■ **Relax the Back Store**
www.relaxtheback.com/

■ **Revo**
www.revo.com

■ **Rock Shox**
www.rockshox.com/flash.html

■ **Rolling Pin Kitchen Emporium**
www.rollingpin.com/

■ **Rubber Baby Buggy Bumpers**
www.rubberbaby.com/

■ **Shaker Furniture**
ncnet.com/ncnw/gall-shr.html

■ **Shoes on the Net**
www.shoesonthenet.com/

■ **Shop Titanic**
maritimeheritage.com/

■ **Snookie's Cookies**
www.snookies.com/

■ **Southpaw Enterprizes**
www.southpaw.bc.ca/

■ **Sovietski Collection**
www.sovietski.com/

■ **Specialty Linens**
www.specialty-linens.com/

■ **Submarine Memorabilia**
www.subshipstore.com/

■ **SunglassSource**
www.eyeglassplace.com/sunglasses/

■ **Swiss Army Brands**
www.swissarmy.com

■ **Texas Branding Company**
www.cowboys.com/texasbrandingironco/

■ **Time by Design**
timebydesign.com/

■ **Unclaimed Baggage**
www.unclaimedbaggage.com/

■ **Violet**
www.violet.com/

■ **Vitamin Shoppe**
www.vitaminshoppe.com/

■ **Walkabout Travel Gear**
www.walkabouttravelgear.com/

■ **Way Out West**
www.wayoutwest.com/

■ **Wig Outlet**
www.wigs.com/

■ **Wind-up Toys**
www.winduptoyco.com/

Sounds

Some of these sites have serious information about adding sound to an Internet site. Some, like the Police Scanner, are merely odd uses of sound. But most are examples of how sound can add an extra dimension to a site.

■ **4AD**
www.4ad.com/

■ **Answering Machine**
www.answeringmachine.co.uk/

■ **Audible**
www.audible.com/

■ **Audiocafe**
www.audiocafe.com/

■ **Ballparks**
www.ballparks.com/

■ **Broadcast.com**
www.audionet.com/

■ **Capitol Steps**
www.capsteps.com/

■ **Classical MIDI Archives**
www.prs.net/midi.html

■ **CowPokin' Fun**
www.geocities.com/
~cowpokinfun/
index.htm

■ **Daily Feed**
www.dailyfeed.com/

■ **Daily WAV**
www.dailywav.com/

■ **Fantasy Jazz**
www.fantasyjazz.com

■ **Historical Speeches**
www.webcorp.com/
sounds/index.htm

▲ www.geocities.com/
~cowpokinfun/index.htm

■ **JFK Tapes**
www.c-span.org/ram/jfk/jfk012699_04.ram

■ **Live Concerts**
www.liveconcerts.com

■ **Live-Online**
www.live-online.com/

■ **Lost and Found Sounds**
www.npr.org/programs/lnfsound/

■ **Metaverse**
metaverse.com/

■ **MIDI Home Page**
www.eeb.ele.tue.nl/midi/index.html

■ **Movies Sounds**
 www.moviesounds.com/

■ **MusicMaker**
www.musicmaker.com/

■ **One Stop Jazz**
www.mindspring.com/~kvansant/

■ **One-on-One Sports**
www.1on1sports.com/

■ **Police Scanner**
www.policescanner.com/

■ **RealGuide**
realguide.real.com/

■ **Sites with Audio Clips**
www.geek-girl.com/audioclips.html

■ **Soundbites**
www.soundbites.com/

■ **Sounds Online**
www.soundsonline.com/

■ **Spinner**
www.spinner.com/

■ **Standard MIDI Files**
www.aitech.ac.jp/~ckelly/SMF.html

■ **Subaudio**
www.subaudio.net/

■ **The Moonlit Road**
www.themoonlitroad.com/

■ **The Sound**
www.thesound.com/

■ **The Soundry**
hyperion.advanced.org/19537/

■ **This American Life**
www.thislife.org/

Social Sciences

See also Economics, History, *and* Political Science.

■ **Ancient World Web**
www.julen.net/aw/

■ **Anthropology Biographies**
www.anthro.mankato.msus.edu/bio/

■ **Anthropology Resources on the Internet**
home.worldnet.fr/clist/Anthro/

■ **Archeology on the Net**
www.serve.com/archaeology/main.html

■ **Best Practices Database**
www.bestpractices.org/

■ **Center for Survey Research**
www.fhsu.edu/htmlpages/services/survey/
index.html

■ **Country Studies: Area
Handbook Series**
lcweb2.loc.gov/frd/cs/cshome.html

■ **Demographics**
www.cnie.org/pop/population.htm

■ **Expeditions Online**
www.expeditionresearch.org/english/
exonline/cat/anthropology.html

■ **Indigenous Peoples' Information**
www.halcyon.com/FWDP/

■ **Migration Site**
www.iom.ch/welcome.htm

■ **National Sprawl News Index**
www.interaxs.net/pub/mikemonett/natl.htm

■ **Psychology with Style**
www.uwsp.edu/acad/psych/apa4b.htm

■ **Psychology.net**
www.psychology.net/

■ **Public Opinion Database**
www.ciesin.org/datasets/irss/irss.html

■ **Race and Ethnic Studies Institute**
resi.tamu.edu/index.html

■ **Research Resources for the
Social Sciences**
www.socsciresearch.com/

■ **Shaping Our Communities: The Impact of Information Technology**
www.internetcenter.state.mn.us/ltn-open.htm

■ **Social Psychology Network**
www.wesleyan.edu/spn/

■ **Social Science Data Achives**
osiris.colorado.edu/SOC/RES/data.html

■ **Social Science Directory**
www.tradenet.it/links/arsocu/social.html

■ **Social Statistics Briefing Room**
www.whitehouse.gov/fsbr/ssbr.html

■ **U.S. Demography**
www.ciesin.org/datasets/us-demog/us-demog-home.html

■ **Uncommonly Difficult IQ Tests**
www.eskimo.com/~miyaguch/hoeflin.html

■ **Urban Planning 2010**
cad9.cadlab.umanitoba.ca/jill/up2010.html

■ **Web of Culture**
www.webofculture.com/

Space

Most of these sites, as you might expect, have their origins in NASA. All are informative and many are breathtaking.

■ **Ask an Astronaut**
www.nss.org/askastro/

■ **Astronaut Connection**
nauts.com/

■ **Astronomy Picture of the Day**
antwrp.gsfc.nasa.gov/apod/astropix.html

■ **Cassini: Voyage to Saturn**
www.jpl.nasa.gov/cassini/

■ **Center for Mars Exploration**
cmex-www.arc.nasa.gov/

■ **Deep Cold**
www.deepcold.com/

■ **Earth Images from Space**
code935.gsfc.nasa.gov/Tutorial/TofC/
Coverpage.html

■ **Earthshots**
edcwww.cr.usgs.gov/earthshots/slow/
tableofcontents

■ **Hubble Space Telescope**
quest.arc.nasa.gov/interactive/hst.html/

■ **Mars Society**
www.marssociety.org/

■ **Messier Catalog**
www.seds.org/messier/

■ **NASA Human Spaceflight**
station.nasa.gov/

■ **NASA Observatorium**
observe.ivv.nasa.gov/

■ **NASA Space Center**
www.jsc.nasa.gov/

■ **National Air and Space Museum**
www.nasm.si.edu/

■ **National Space Society**
www.nss.org/

■ **Orion Nebula**
www.naoj.org/outreach/
press_releases/990128

■ **Project Galileo**
www.jpl.nasa.gov/galileo/

■ **Satellite Tracking**
liftoff.msfc.nasa.gov/realtime/jtrack/

■ **Space Library**
samadhi.jpl.nasa.gov/

■ **Space Telescope Science Institute**
www.stsci.edu/

■ **Structure and Evolution of the Universe**
universe.gsfc.nasa.gov/

■ **Top 20 Shoemaker-Levy Images**
www.jpl.nasa.gov/sl9/top20.html

Sports

Sports are one of the most popular categories on the Internet. This is just a tiny sample. You can surely find anything in the field of sports on the Internet.

■ **ActiveUSA**
www.activeusa.com/

■ **All Star Sites**
www.allstarsites.com/

■ **AllSports**
www.allsports.com/index.html

■ **Amateur Sports Net**
thepacificplace.com/asn/index.cfm

■ **Athlete Network**
athletenetwork.com/

■ **Atlantic Endeavor**
www.ariadne.net/atlantic_endeavour/

■ **Baseball Time Machine**
www.exploratorium.edu/baseball/
timemachine.html

■ **Basketball Server**
www4.nando.net/SportServer/basketball/

■ **Coaching Science Abstracts**
www-rohan.sdsu.edu/dept/coachsci/
index.htm

■ **College Sports News Daily**
chili.collegesportsnews.com/default.htm

■ **College Sports Online**
www.collegesports-online.com/

■ **Cool Running**
www.coolrunning.com/

■ **CyberPump**
www.cyberpump.com/

■ **ESPNet SportsZone**
espnet.sportszone.com/

■ **Extreme Sports**
www.extremesports.com/

■ **Fans Only**
www.fansonly.com/

■ **Figure Skaters' Website**
www.webcom.com/dnkorte/sk8_0000.html

■ **Freestyle Frisbee**
www.frisbee.com/

■ **GolfWeb**
www.golfweb.com

■ **GoSki**
www.goski.com/

■ **Gymn**
gymn.digiweb.com/gymn/

■ **Hockey Over Time**
www.lcshockey.com/history/

■ **Iditarod Dog Sled Race**
www.alaskanet.com/iditarod/

■ **Internet Football League**
www.internetfootball.com/

■ **Jump Roping**
www.usajrf.org/

■ **National Hotrod Association**
www.nhraonline.com/

■ **NCAA News**
www.ncaa.org/news/

■ **NFL Fantasy**
www.best.com/~football/football.html

■ **Olympic Movement**
www.olympic.org/

■ **On Hoops**
www.onhoops.com/

▲ www.onhoops.com

■ **Planet Sport**
www.sextant.it/fs/

■ **Rollerblade**
www.rollerblade.com/

■ **Sailing Source**
paw.com/sail/

■ **Science of Baseball**
www.exploratorium.edu/baseball/

■ **ScubaDuba**
www.scubaduba.com/

■ **Skate City**
www.skatecity.com/

■ **SkateWeb**
frog.simplenet.com/skateweb/

■ **SkiNet**
www.iski.com/

■ **Skydive Archive**
www.afn.org/skydive/

■ **Slam Duncan**
www.slamduncan.com/index.html

■ **Snowboarding Online**
www.twsnow.com/

■ **SnoWeb**
www.snoweb.com

■ **SoccerNet**
soccernet.com/

■ **Sporting News**
www.sportingnews.com/

■ **Sports Gateway**
www.sportsgateway.com/

■ **Sports Illustrated**
cnnsi.com/

■ **Stadiums and Arenas**
www.wwcd.com/stadiums.html

■ **Surf Check**
www.surfcheck.com/

■ **Tennis Country**
www.tenniscountry.com

■ **Total Baseball**
www.totalbaseball.com/

■ **Total Sports**
www.totalsports.net/

■ **Triathlete**
www.triathletemag.com/index.html

■ **U.S. Masters Diving**
www.n2.net/diving/

■ **United States Swimming**
www.usswim.org/

■ **USA Gymnastics Online**
www.usa-gymnastics.org/

■ **USA National Rugby Team**
www.usa-eagles.org/

■ **USA Track and Field**
www.usatf.org/index.htm

■ **VolleyballSeek**
www.volleyballseek.com/

■ **Water Zone**
members.aol.com/adstring/water.htm

■ **WeightsNet**
www.weightsnet.com/

■ **Windsurfer.com**
www.windsurfer.com/

■ **World Wide Web of Sports**
www.tns.lcs.mit.edu/cgi-bin/sports

■ **Your League**
www.yourleague.com/

States

Most states offer many sites, especially related to tourism. The ones listed here are, for the most part, the "official" sites. Some are strictly governmental, but most are broader in scope.

■ **Alabama**
www.state.al.us/

■ **Alaska**
www.state.ak.us/

■ **Arizona**
www.state.az.us/

States

- **Arkansas**
www.state.ar.us/
- **California**
www.ca.gov/s/
- **Colorado**
www.state.co.us/
- **Connecticut**
www.state.ct.us/
- **Delaware**
www.state.de.us/
- **Florida**
originalflorida.org/
- **Georgia**
www.state.ga.us/
- **Hawaii**
www.hawaii.net/cgi-bin/hhp?
- **Idaho**
www.state.id.us/
- **Illinois**
www.state.il.us/
- **Indiana**
www.state.in.us/
- **Iowa**
www.state.ia.us/index.html
- **Kansas**
www.state.ks.us/
- **Kentucky**
www.state.ky.us/

■ **Louisiana**
www.wisdom.com/la/la1.htm

■ **Maine**
janus.state.me.us/homepage.asp

■ **Maryland**
www.state.md.us/

■ **Massachusetts**
www.magnet.state.ma.us/

■ **Michigan**
www.state.mi.us/

■ **Minnesota**
www.state.mn.us/

■ **Mississippi**
www.state.ms.us/

■ **Missouri**
www.state.mo.us/

■ **Montana**
www.state.mt.us/

■ **Nebraska**
www.state.ne.us/

■ **Nevada**
www.state.nv.us/

■ **New Hampshire**
www.state.nh.us/

■ **New Jersey**
www.state.nj.us/

■ **New Mexico**
www.state.nm.us/

- **New York**
www.state.ny.us/
- **North Carolina**
www.state.nc.us/
- **North Dakota**
www.state.nd.us/
- **Ohio**
www.ohio.gov/
- **Oklahoma**
www.oklaosf.state.ok.us/
- **Oregon**
www.state.or.us/
- **Pennsylvania**
www.state.pa.us/
- **Rhode Island**
visitrhodeisland.com/
- **South Carolina**
www.state.sc.us/
- **South Dakota**
www.state.sd.us/
- **Tennessee**
www.state.tn.us/
- **Texas**
www.state.tx.us/
- **Utah**
www.state.ut.us/
- **Vermont**
www.state.vt.us/

■ **Virginia**
www.state.va.us/

■ **Washington**
access.wa.gov/

■ **West Virginia**
www.state.wv.us/

■ **Wisconsin**
www.state.wi.us/

■ **Wyoming**
www.state.wy.us/

Statistics

Some pretty interesting stuff here. Statistics, as presented to the public, definitely are not boring.

■ **Consumer Price Indexes**
stats.bls.gov/cpihome.htm

■ **Criminal Justice Statistics**
www.albany.edu/sourcebook/

■ **Demography and Population Studies**
coombs.anu.edu.au/ResFacilities/
DemographyPage.html

■ **Fedstats**
www.fedstats.gov/

■ **GlobalStatistics**
www.stats.demon.nl/

■ Journal of Statistics Education
www2.ncsu.edu/ncsu/pams/stat/info/jse/
homepage.html

■ Justice Statistics
www.ojp.usdoj.gov/bjs/

■ Labor Statistics
stats.bls.gov

■ National Highway Traffic Safety
www.nhtsa.dot.gov/

■ Statistical Methodology
www.bts.gov/fcsm/

**■ Statistics Every Writer
Should Know**
nilesonline.com/stats/

■ StatLib Index
temper.stat.cmu.edu/

■ Stat-USA
www.stat-usa.gov/

■ Transportation Statistics
www.bts.gov/

■ U.S. Census Bureau
www.census.gov/

■ World Population
sunsite.unc.edu/lunarbin/worldpop

Streaming

Hear it and see it, directly from the Internet.

Streaming

■ **15 Minutes**
www.zeldman.com/15/

■ **ChannelSeek**
channelseek.com/

■ **Indiana Jones Streaming Video**
indyjones.simplenet.com/video/video.htm

■ **Internet Radio Stations**
radiotower.com/internetradio/liveaudio.asp

■ **Rolling Stone Radio**
www.rsradio.com/home/

■ **SHOUTcast**
www.shoutcast.com/download.html

■ **Streaming Independent Music and Video**
www.nolabel.com/index.html

■ **Streaming Media World**
streamingmediaworld.com/

■ **Streaming Solutions**
www.ss-i.com/

■ **TV on the Web**
www.tvontheweb.com/

■ **Zone Radio**
www.mountainzone.com/radio/

Taxes

There may be something helpful here for individuals or businesses.

■ **Ecological Tax Reform Studies**
www.tellus.org/e-taxref.html

■ **Estate and Gift Tax Law**
www.law.cornell.edu/topics/
estate_gift_tax.html

■ **Flat Tax Home Page**
flattax.house.gov/

■ **Glossary of Tax and
Accounting Terms**
www.mcn.org/A/MGCO/glossary.htm

■ **IRS Tax Terms**
www.irs.ustreas.gov/prod/taxi/taxterms.
html

■ **Nolo's Legal Encyclopedia—
Tax problems**
www.nolo.com/ChunkTAX/TAX.index.html

■ **Sports, Jobs, and Taxes**
www.brook.edu/pub/review/summer97/
noll.htm

■ **Tax Analysts Online**
www.tax.org/

■ **Tax Freedom Institute**
www.taxhelponline.com/tfihome.htm

■ **Tax Prophet**
www.taxprophet.com/

■ **Tax Resources**
www.taxresources.com/

■ **Tax Season Survival Kit**
freedom.house.gov/survival/

■ **Tax Tables**
www.irs.ustreas.gov/prod/ind_info/
tax_tables/index.html

■ **Tax Web**
www.taxweb.com/

■ **Tax World**
www.taxworld.org/

■ **TaxHelpOnline**
www.taxhelponline.com/

■ **TaxLinks**
www.taxlinks.com/

■ **U.S. Tax Code Online**
www.fourmilab.ch/ustax/ustax.html

Techie Company Sites

Makers of hardware and software. Their sites better be cool, right? Also, if you are looking for a job in the computer field, these sites often describe openings and solicit applications.

■ **3COM**
www.3com.com/

■ **Adaptec**
www.adaptec.com/

■ **Adobe Systems**
www.adobe.com/

■ **America Online**
www.aol.com/

■ **American Micro Devices**
www.amd.com/

■ **Apple**
www.apple.com

■ **Autodesk**
www.autodesk.com

■ **Baan**
www.baan.com

■ **Banyan**
www.banyan.com

■ **Borland**
www.borland.com/

■ **Brightpoint**
www.brightpoint.com/static/global/global.htm

■ **Broderbund**
www.broderbund.com/

■ **Cisco**
www.cisco.com/

■ **Citrix Systems**
www.citrix.com/

■ **Claris**
www.claris.com

■ **Compaq**
www.compaq.com/

■ **Computer Associates**
www.cai.com/

■ **Corel**
www.corel.com/

■ **Cyrix**
www.cyrix.com

■ **Dell**
www.dell.com/

■ **DoubleClick**
www.doubleclick.net

■ **Firefly**
www.firefly.com/

■ **Gateway**
www.gateway.com/

■ **Hewlett-Packard**
www.hp.com/

■ **Inktomi**
www.inktomi.com/

■ **Intel**
www.intel.com/

■ **Iomega**
www.iomega.com/

■ **Lucent**
www.lucent.com

■ **Metatools**
www.metatools.com

■ **Micron**
www.micron.com/

■ **Microsoft**
www.microsoft.com/

■ **Morning Star Technologies**
www.morningstar.com/

■ **Motorola**
www.mot.com/

■ **National Semiconductor**
www.national.com/

■ **NEC**
www.nec.com

■ **NetObjects**
www.netobjects.com

■ **Pixar**
www.pixar.com/

■ **Quantum**
www.quantum.com/

■ **SAP**
www.sap.com/

■ **Shiva**
www.shiva.com

■ **Sierra**
www.sierra.com/

■ **Sun Microsystems**
www.sun.com/

■ **Symantic**
www.symantec.com/

■ **Texas Instrument**
www.ti.com/

■ **Trilogy**
www.trilogy.com/

■ **Veritas**
www.veritas.com

■ **Vitesse**
www.vitesse.com/

■ **Wind River**
www.windriver.com/

Television

The premiere shows and the major networks have their own sites. The other sites include listings, reviews, and historical perspectives.

■ **Academy of Television Arts
and Sciences**
www.emmys.org/

■ **Ad Critic**
www.adcritic.com/

■ **American Movie Classics**
www.amctv.com/

■ **Antiques Roadshow**
www.pbs.org/wgbh/pages/roadshow/
home.html

■ **Austin Cyber Limits**
www.pbs.org/klru/austin/

■ **Best Bits of Britcom**
britcom.interspeed.net/

■ **Biography**
www.biography.com/

■ **Black Entertainment Network**
www.betnetworks.com/

■ **CNN Interactive**
www.cnn.com/

■ **Computer Chronicles**
www.cmptv.com/computerchronicles/

■ **Court TV Famous Cases**
www.courttv.com/famous/

■ **C-SPAN**
www.c-span.org/

■ **Discovery Channel**
www.discovery.com/

■ **Episode Guides Page**
www.xnet.com/~djk/main_page.shtml

■ **E! Online**
www.eonline.com/

■ **Free TV Tickets**
www.tvtix.com/

■ **Frontline**
www2.pbs.org/wgbh/pages/frontline/

■ **Gist**
www.thegist.com/

■ **Golden Age of Television**
www.aentv.com/home/golden/goldtv.htm

■ **History Channel**
www.historychannel.com/

■ **Infomercial Index**
www.magickeys.com/infomercials/

■ **Lifetime Online**
www.lifetimetv.com/

■ **MSNBC**
www.msnbc.com/

■ **Nielsen Media Research**
www.nielsenmedia.com/

■ **NOVA Online**
www.pbs.org/wgbh/nova/

■ **PBS Online**
www.pbs.org/

■ **Primetime Review**
www.primetimereview.com/

■ **Quizsite**
www.quizsite.com/

■ **RockOnTV**
www.rockontv.com/

■ **Soap Opera Central**
www.amcpages.com/soapcentral/

■ **TV Barn**
www.tvbarn.com/

■ **TV Collectables**
www.jimtvc.com/

■ **TV Guide**
www.tvguide.com/

■ **TV-Ultra**
www.tvultra.com/

■ **Ultimate TV**
www.ultimatetv.com/

■ **Unsolved Mysteries**
www.unsolved.com/missing.html

■ **Yesterdayland**
www.yesterdayland.com/

Testing

If you need to take any kind of test for academic admission, help is as close as your computer. This list includes the official sites of the test makers and several for folks who would like to help you, usually for a fee.

■ **ACT Assessment**
www.act.org

■ **Berkeley Review MCAT Prep**
www.berkeley-review.com/

■ **College Board Online**
www.collegeboard.org/

■ **College PowerPrep**
www.powerprep.com/

■ **Columbia Review MCAT Prep**
www.columbiareview.com/

■ **Educational Testing
Service Network**
www.ets.org/

■ **GMAT Coaching**
www.angelfire.com/biz/gmatcoaching/
gmat.html

■ **GoCollege**
www.gocollege.com/

■ **GRE Test Prep**
4testprep.com/gre/

■ **Kaplan: Test Yourself**
www.kaplan.com/library/testself.html

■ **Law School Admission Council LSAT**
www.lsac.org/

■ **Lighthouse Review**
www.lighthousereview.com/

■ **LSAT Intelligent Solutions**
www.gate.net/~tutor/

Theatre

What's on, who's playing, what's good, what isn't—it's all here.

■ **Actors Web**
starone.com/actorsweb/

■ **American Cabaret Theatre**
www.americancabarettheatre.com/Theatre/
about.html

■ **American Theater Web**
www.americantheaterweb.com/

■ **Broadway Theater Online**
www.broadwaytheater.com/

■ **Broadway Theatre Archive**
www.tbta.com/home.html

■ **Carnegie Hall**
www.carnegiehall.org/

Theatre

■ **Costume Source**
www.milieux.com/costume/source.html

■ **Family Theater Guide**
nyctourist.com/bway_familyguide.htm

■ **Glossary of Technical Theatre Terms**
www.ex.ac.uk/drama/tech/glossary.html

■ **History of Costumes**
www.siue.edu/COSTUMES/history.html

■ **Improv Page**
sunee.uwaterloo.ca/~broehl/improv/

■ **London Theatre Guide**
www.londontheatre.co.uk/

■ **Musicals Net**
musicals.net/

■ **On Broadway**
artsnet.heinz.cmu.edu/OnBroadway/

■ **Playbill**
www1.playbill.com/playbill/

■ **Shakespeare and the Globe**
starone.com/actorsweb/

■ **Stage Directions Magazine**
www.stage-directions.com/

■ **Talkin' Broadway**
www.talkinbroadway.com/

■ **Theater Jobs Online**
theatrejobs.com/

■ **Theater Sites**
artsnet.heinz.cmu.edu/Artsites/Theater.html

■ **Theatre Perspectives International**
www.tesser.com/tpi/

■ **Tony Awards**
www.tonys.org/

■ **What's On Stage**
www.whatsonstage.com/

Travel—Destinations, Adventures, and Attractions

As is so often true in regard to the Internet, this list is just a small sample. If you have a specific destination in mind, you can surely find several sites that tell you anything you would like to know.

■ **10 Downing Street**
www.number-10.gov.uk/

■ **360 Alaska**
www.360alaska.com/index.htm

■ **Adventure Destinations**
www.adventuredestinations.com/

■ **Air Courier Travel**
www.jps.net/nickstas/

■ **Alaska Ferries**
www.akms.com/ferry/

■ **All Aboard the Silver Streak**
www.ping.be/~ping0420/

■ **America's Roof**
www.americasroof.com/

■ **Backroads Traveler**
www.backroads.com/

■ **Balloons over New England**
www.pbpub.com/ballooning/index.html

■ **Beaches and Islands**
travel.epicurious.com/traveler/
great_escapes/great_escapes.html

■ **Bellringing at Canterbury Cathedral**
web.ukonline.co.uk/Members/mark.gilham/
cathedral/index.htm

■ **Best Beaches**
www.petrix.com/beaches/

■ **Betsy Ross House**
www.libertynet.org/iha/betsy/

■ **Bird Treks**
www.birdtreks.com/

■ **Botanical Gardens**
www.helsinki.fi/kmus/botgard.html

■ **California Shipwreck Database**
ourworld.compuserve.com/homepages/
WRECK_DIVER/database.htm

■ **CityView**
www.cityview.com/

■ **Colorado Vacation Adventures**
www.abwam.com/wedgwood/
vacation.html

■ **Country Walkers**
countrywalkers.com/

■ **Covered Bridges**
william-king.www.drexel.edu/top/bridge/
CB1.html

■ **Crazy Dog Travel Guide**
www.infomatch.com/~cdtg/

■ **Crazy Horse**
www.crazyhorse.org/

■ **EarthWise Journeys**
www.teleport.com/~earthwyz/index.htm

■ **European Walking Tours**
www.gorp.com/ewt/

■ **Fall in Pennsylvania**
www.fallinpa.com/

■ **Freighter Cruises**
www.freighterworld.com/

■ **Ghost Towns**
www.cultimedia.ch/ghosttowns/

■ **Graceland**
www.elvis-presley.com/

■ **Hamptons**
www.thehamptons.com/

■ **Hawaii**
www.visit.hawaii.org/

■ **Hearst Castle**
www.hearstcastle.org/

■ **Hidden America**
www.hiddenamerica.com/

■ **Hidden Trails**
www.hiddentrails.com/

■ **Hostel Links**
www.ping.be/~ping0420/

■ **Learning Vacations**
www.learningvacations.com/

■ **Legendary Lighthouses**
www.pbs.org/legendarylighthouses/

■ **Lift Hill**
www.lifthill.com/

■ **Mardi Gras**
usacitylink.com/mardigr/default.html

■ **Montana High Country
Cattle Drive**
www.iigi.com/os/montana/cattledr/
cattledr.htm

■ **Monterey Bay Aquarium**
www.mbayaq.org/

■ **Moss Springs Packing**
www.iigi.com/os/oregon/moss/vacation.
htm

■ **Mount Rushmore**
www.libertynet.org/iha/betsy/

■ **Mysterious Places**
mysteriousplaces.com/

■ **National Register of Historic Places**
www.cr.nps.gov/nr/

■ **Nature Tours**
naturetour.com/

■ **New England Winding Roads**
miraclemile.com/windingroads/

■ **OK Corral**
www.ok-corral.com/

■ **Old Sturbridge Village**
www.osv.org/

■ **OnSafari**
www.onsafari.com/

■ **Orient Express**
www.orient-expresstrains.com/

■ **Participate in Archeology**
www.cr.nps.gov/aad/particip.htm

■ **Public Aquariums**
www.actwin.com/fish/public.cgi

■ **Ranch Vacations**
www.travelsource.com/ranches/

■ **Ranchweb**
www.ranchweb.com/

■ **Rollercoasters**
www.rollercoaster.com/

■ **Roman Monuments**
www.roma2000.it/zmonum2.
html#Monumenti

■ **Scenic Byways**
www.byways.org/

■ **South Georgia Island**
www.pbs.org/edens/southgeorgia/

■ **South Pole Adventure**
www.southpole.com/

■ **Spa Finder**
www.spafinders.com/

■ **Swimmers Guide**
lornet.com/~SGOL/

■ **Taj Mahal**
www.angelfire.com/in/myindia/
tajmahal.html

■ **The Big Duck**
www.newsday.com/az/bigduck.htm

■ **The Ice**
www.io.com/~pml/welcome.html

■ **Travel @ the Speed of light**
vanbc.wimsey.com/~ayoung/travel.shtml

■ **Ventura Expeditions**
www.subnet.co.uk/ventura/

■ **Wall Drug**
www.state.sd.us/state/executive/tourism/
adds/walldrug.htm

■ **Whale Watching**
www.physics.helsinki.fi/whale/

■ **Wild-Eyed Alaska**
www.hhmi.org/alaska/

■ **World Federation of Great Towers**
www.great-towers.com/

- **World Wide Events**
wwevents.com/

- **World's Largest
Roadside Attractions**
www.infomagic.com/~martince/index.htm

Travel—Planning Information

Anything related to travel, from checking out an obscure location to making airline reservations, can be found on the Internet.

- **Accessible Journeys**
www.disabilitytravel.com/

- **Air Travel Complaints**
www.airtravelcomplaints.com/

- **Airline Toll-Free Numbers**
www.princeton.edu/Main/air800.html

- **All by Word of Mouse**
wordofmouse.com/

- **All Hotels on the Web**
www.all-hotels.com/

- **American Sightseeing International**
www.sightseeing.com/

- **American Student Travel**
www.astravel.com/

- **Amtrak**
www.amtrak.com/

- **Bed and Breakfast Inns**
cimarron.net/

■ **BizTravel**
www.biztravel.com/

■ **CitySearch**
www.citysearch.com/

■ **Civilized Explorer**
www.cieux.com/

■ **Cruise Ship Opinion**
www.cruiseopinion.com/

■ **Currency Converter**
www.olsen.ch/cgi-bin/exmenu

■ **Discount Airfares**
www.aesu.com/

■ **Escape Artist**
www.escapeartist.com/

■ **Escapees RV Club**
www.channel1.com/users/escapees/

■ **European Railway Server**
mercurio.iet.unipi.it/home.html

■ **Foreign Languages for Travelers**
www.travlang.com/languages/

■ **Frommer's Outspoken Encyclopedia of Travel**
www.frommers.com/

■ **Get Cruising**
www.getcruising.com/

■ **Guide to Bed and Breakfast Inns**
www.ultranet.com/biz/inns/

■ **Guide to Sleeping in Airports**
www3.sympatico.ca/donna.mcsherry/
airports.htm

■ **Hostels of Europe**
www.hostelseurope.com/

■ **Hotel Discounts**
www.hoteldiscount.com/

■ **How to See the World**
www.artoftravel.com/index.html

■ **Innkeeper**
www.theinnkeeper.com/

■ **Insiders' Guides**
www.insiders.com/

■ **International Vacation Homes**
www.ivacation.com/

■ **Lonely Planet**
www.lonelyplanet.com/

■ **Microsoft Expedia**
www.expedia.msn.com

■ **National Travel Exchange**
www.travelx.com/

■ **O Solo Mio**
www.osolomio.com/

■ **Opinionated Traveler**
www.opinionatedtraveler.com/

■ **Passenger Rights**
www.passengerrights.com/

■ **Passport Services**
travel.state.gov/passport_services.html

■ **Priceline**
www.priceline.com/

■ **Rec.Travel Library**
www.Travel-Library.com/

■ **Roadside America**
www.roadsideamerica.com/

■ **Rough Guides**
www.hotwired.com/rough/

■ **Secret Offers**
bestdeals.tytek.net/

■ **See the World on $25 a Day**
www.artoftravel.com/

■ **Shoestring Travel**
www.stratpub.com/

■ **StayWhere**
www.staywhere.com/

■ **TheTrip**
www.thetrip.com/

■ **Third World Traveler**
www.thirdworldtraveler.com/

■ **Tourist Offices Worldwide**
www.mbnet.mb.ca/lucas/travel/
tourism-offices.html

■ **Travel Connection**
www.travelxn.com/

■ **TravelFile**
tfsrvr.travelfile.com/

■ **Traveling with Children**
rainforest.parentsplace.com/dialog/get/
travel.html

■ **Travelocity**
www.travelocity.com/

■ **Travelzoo**
www.travelzoo.com/

■ **U.S. State Home Pages**
www.globalcomputing.com/states.html

■ **U.S. State Department
Travel Warnings**
travel.state.gov/travel_warnings.html

■ **USA CityLink**
banzai.neosoft.com/citylink/

■ **United States of America Page**
sunsite.unc.edu/usa/usahome.html

■ **Vacation Rental Source**
www.vrsource.com/

■ **Virtual Tourist**
www.vtourist.com/

■ **Wanderlust**
www.americanexpress.com/student/
wander/wander.html

■ **Web Travel Review**
photo.net/webtravel/

■ **WebFlyer**
www.webflyer.com/

■ **World's Most Dangerous Places**
www.fieldingtravel.com/df/index.htm

■ **Worldwide Brochures**
www.wwb.com/main.html

Travel—Restaurant Guides

Around the world or down the street—you have to eat somewhere.

■ **ActiveDiner**
www.activediner.com/HomePage.cfm

■ **Celebrity Fare**
pathfinder.com/people/celebrityfare/

■ **Chowhound**
www.chowhound.com/

■ **Cuisine.Net**
www.dinnerandamovie.com/

■ **Dine.com**
www.dine.com/

■ **Diner City**
www.dinercity.com/

■ **Diners' Grapevine World Restaurant Guide**
www.dinersgrapevine.com/

■ **Dinner and a Movie**
www.dinnerandamovie.com/

■ **Eat Here**
www.eathere.com/

■ **Eat in Germany**
www.eat-germany.net/

■ **EatNet**
www.eatnet.com/

■ **Ethiopean Restaurants around the Globe**
www.nh.ultranet.com/~wube/
Location7.html

■ **Fodor's Restaurant Index**
www.fodors.com/ri.cgi

■ **Food Plex**
www.gigaplex.com/food/index.htm

■ **Indian Restaurants**
secondary.blueshift.com/indrest/Content/
HomePage.asp

■ **Kosher Restaurant Database**
shamash.org/kosher/

■ **Restaurant Row**
www.restaurantrow.
com/

■ **Roadside Online**
www.roadsidemagazine.
com/

■ **Savvy Diner Restaurant Guide**
www.savvydiner.com/

▲ www.savvydiner.com/

■ **Sushi World Guide**
www.sushi.infogate.de/

■ **Ultimate Restaurant Directory**
www.orbweavers.com/ULTIMATE/

■ **Unione Ristoranti del Buon Ricordo**
www.pantarei.it/buonricordo/

■ **United States Dining Guide**
shamash.org/kosher/

■ **Washington, D.C., Restaurants**
www.washingtonian.com/dining/

■ **World Guide to Vegetarian Restaurants**
www.veg.org/veg/Guide/

■ **WorldMenus**
www.worldmenus.com/

Travel—Virtual Tours

Go anywhere but stay where you are. These sites give the feeling of the trip without having to pack a bag.

■ **Acapulco Virtual Tour**
www.acapulco-virtual.com/

■ **American Red Cross Virtual Museum**
www.redcross.org/hec/index.html

■ **Amsterdam Virtual Tour**
www.channels.nl/

■ **Animal Kingdom Virtual Tour**
members.tripod.com/adm/popup/
roadmap.shtml

■ **Around the World in 80 Clicks**
www.coolsite.com/arworld.html

■ **Assissi Virtual Tour**
www.assind.perugia.it/umbria/assisi/

■ **Belize Virtual Tour**
www.travelbelize.org/guide/guidehp.html

■ **Boeing Virtual Tour**
www.boeing.com/companyoffices/gallery/
video/

■ **Budapest Virtual Tour**
www.budapest.com/

■ **Castles on the Web**
www.castlesontheweb.com/

■ **Cyprus Virtual Tour**
www.channels.nl/

■ **Great Wall of China Virtual Tour**
www.chinavista.com/travel/greatwall/
greatwall.html

■ **Ireland Virtual Tour**
www.thevirtualwall.org/

■ **Istanbul Virtual Tour**
www.ddg.com/ISTANBUL/

■ **Jamaica Virtual Tour**
www.virtualjamaica.com/

■ **Jerusalem Virtual Tour**
www.md.huji.ac.il/vjt/

■ **Lizzie Borden House Virtual Tour**
www.halfmoon.org/borden/

■ **Mendenhall Glacier Virtual Tour**
www.snowcrest.net/geography/field/
mendenhall/index.html

■ **Miami Virtual Tour**
www.miamivr.com/

■ **Moscow Virtual Tour**
www.miamivr.com/

■ **Nairobi Virtual Tour**
www.kenyaweb.com/vnairobi/town.html

■ **National Civil Rights Museum
Virtual Tour**
www.mecca.org/~crights/cyber.html

■ **New Zealand Virtual Tour**
www.nz.com/tour/

■ **Norfolk Island Virtual Tour**
www.nz.com/tour/

■ **Pompeii Forum Project**
jefferson.village.virginia.edu/pompeii/
page-1.html

■ **San Diego Model Railroad
Virtual Tour**
www.globalinfo.com/noncomm/SDMRM/
sdmrm.html

■ **Sistine Chapel**
www.christusrex.org/www1/sistine/
0-Tour.html

■ **Sugar Loaf Virtual Tour**
www.bondinho.com.br/

■ **Torquay**
www.halien.com/tour/Torquay/intro.htm

■ **Tower of London Virtual Tour**
www.toweroflondontour.com/

■ **Venice Virtual Tour**
www.virtualvenice.com/

■ **Virtual Field Trips**
www.field-guides.com/

■ **Virtual HoJo**
ic.net/~dover/hojo.htm

■ **Virtual Road Trip**
virtualroadtrip.com/

■ **Yemen Virtual Tour**
www.yemennet.com/tour/yemen.htm

Useful Stuff

And we mean really *useful. No esoteric computer stuff, just the info we need on occasion.*

■ **800 Phone Numbers**
www.inter800.com/

■ **Ability Utility**
www.learn2.com/

■ **Area Code Lookup**
www.555-1212.com/ACLOOKUP.HTML

Useful Stuff

■ **Ask an Expert**
www.askanexpert.com/askanexpert/

■ **Calculator.com**
www.calculator.com/

■ **Coin Flipping**
shazam.econ.ubc.ca/flip/

■ **Convert It!**
www.microimg.com/science/

■ **Credit Score Secrets**
creditscoring.com/

■ **Department of Motor Vehicles**
www.ameri.com/dmv/dmv.htm

■ **Disabilities Information Resources**
www.dinf.org/

■ **Electronic Ticket Exchange**
www.tixs.com/

■ **Freedom of Information Request**
www.rcfp.org/foi_lett.html

■ **How Far Is It?**
www.indo.com/distance/

■ **How Stuff Works**
www.howstuffworks.com/

■ **Lost and Found**
www.lost-and-found.com/

■ **Megaconverter**
www.megaconverter.com/

■ **New York Subway Instruction Page**
www.juvenilemedia.com/subway/

■ **PostagePlus**
www.postageplus.com

■ **Reverse Telephone Directory**
www.anywho.com/telq.html

■ **Speedtrap Registry**
www.speedtrap.com/speedtrap/

■ **Toll-Free Number Directory**
www.tollfree.att.net/dir800/

■ **Traffic Waves**
www.eskimo.com/~billb/amateur/traffic/
traffic1.html

■ **Useful Site of the Day**
www.zdnet.com/yil/content/depts/useful/
useful.html

■ **VCR Repair**
www.fixer.com/

■ **Wacky Uses**
www.wackyuses.com/

■ **World Clock**
www.timeanddate.com/worldclock/

■ **Zip Code Lookup**
www.usps.gov/ncsc/

Virtual Community

Each of these sites have multiple and varied offerings. But the main attraction is some sort of user connection, usually in the form of live chat.

- **Asian Avenue**
www.communityconnect.com/AsianAvenue.html

- **BizWomen**
www.bizwomen.com/

- **Black Voices**
www.blackvoices.com/

- **Café de Paris**
paris-anglo.com/cafe/

- **Caribbean City**
www.caribbeancity.com/

- **Chat Planet**
www.chatplanet.com/

- **Cloud City**
www.angelfire.com/ny/acloud/

- **CNN Community Discussion**
cnn.com/discussion/

- **College Club**
www.collegeclub.com/members/

- **Cultural Café**
www.languageconnect.com/cafe/

- **Cybercafes Worldwide**
www.netcafeguide.com/

- **Delphi Forum**
www.delphi.com/

- **Electric Minds**
www.minds.com/

- **FolksOnline**
www.folksonline.com/

■ **IVillage**
www.ivillage.com/

■ **LatinoLink**
www.latinolink.com/

■ **LostWorlds**
www.lost-worlds.com/

■ **Rain Web**
www.rain.org

■ **Reality Check**
www.realitycheck.com/

▲ serendip.brynmawr.edu/

■ **Serendip**
serendip.brynmawr.edu/

■ **Talk City**
www.talkcity.com/

■ **Tap Online Community**
www.taponline.com/

■ **Teen.com**
www.teen.com/

■ **The Palace**
www.thepalace.com

■ **The Well**
www.well.com/

■ **Tribal Voice**
www.tribal.com/

■ **World Village**
www.worldvillage.com/

■ **Worlds Away**
www.worldsaway.com/

■ **Y'all**
www.accessatlanta.com/global/local/yall/

Volunteer Vacations

Not sure about a two-year commitment to the Peace Corps? Try a volunteer vacation first.

■ **4Volunteeer**
www.crossculturalsolutions.org/
projectindia/vlntr_abrd.html

■ **Adventurequest: Habitat for Humanity**
www.adventurequest.com/region/
nicaragua.htm

■ **Amizade Volunteer Vacations**
amizade.org/programs.htm

■ **Other Adventures: Volunteer Vacations**
www.mountwashingtonvalley.com/
top-of-the-world/other4.html

■ **Sousson Foundation**
www.sousson.org/students.html

■ **Start Thinking About a Volunteer Vacation**
www.ihad.org/

■ **Volunteer Abroad**
www.crossculturalsolutions.org/
projectindia/vlntr_abrd.html

■ **Volunteer America Vacations**
www.volunteeramerica.com/
VolVacations.htm

■ **Volunteer and Eco-Tourism
Vacations**
www.dtour.com/

■ **Volunteer Vacations: The Book**
www.ipgbook.com/press/vova1.htm

Weather

*If you need to know now, the Internet is your
fastest and most complete weather source.*

■ **Accuweather**
www.accuweather.com/

■ **BBC Weather Centre**
www.bbc.co.uk/weather/

■ **CNN Weather**
www.cnn.com/WEATHER/

■ **Current Atlantic Tropical Storms**
www.solar.ifa.hawaii.edu/Tropical/Gif/atl.
latest.gif

■ **EarthWatch Weather on Demand**
www.earthwatch.com/

■ **Hurricane Hunters**
www.hurricanehunters.com/welcome.htm

■ **Intellicast**
www.intellicast.com/

■ **Interactive Weather Information Network**
iwin.nws.noaa.gov/iwin/main.html

■ **National Climatic Data Center**
www.ncdc.noaa.gov/

■ **National Hurricane Center**
www.nhc.noaa.gov/

■ **National Warnings Area**
iwin.nws.noaa.gov/iwin/
nationalwarnings.html

■ **Natural Disaster Reference Database**
ltpwww.gsfc.nasa.gov/ndrd/

■ **Tropical Storm Watch**
www.fema.gov/fema/trop.htm

■ **Twister Chasers**
www.indirect.com/www/storm5/
tchomepage.html

■ **Unisys Weather**
weather.unisys.com/

■ **Weather Advisory**
weather.terrapin.com/

■ **Weather and Climate Image Maps**
grads.iges.org/pix/head.html

■ **Weather by E-Mail**
www.webbers.com/weather/

■ **Weather Channel**
www.weather.com/twc/homepage.twc

■ **Weather24**
www.weather24.com/

Weddings

Surely you wouldn't plan your wedding on your own, not when so many folks on the Internet want to help.

■ **Affectionately Yours**
www.affectionately-yours.com/

■ **And the Bride Wore**
www.visi.com/~dheaton/bride/
the_bride_wore.html

■ **Bridal Gallery**
www.shewey.com/wedding/index.htm

■ **Hawaiian Island Weddings**
www.maui.net/~weddings/

■ **Internet Wedding Links**
a-wedding.com/

■ **Jasmine Bridal**
www.jasminebridal.com/

■ **Matrimony Mambo**
houston.webpoint.com/wedding/

■ **My Wedding Companion**
users.southeast.net/~fivestar/

■ **New York City Weddings**
www.nycityweddings.com/

■ **Our Special Day**
www.ourspecialday.com/

■ **The Knot**
www4.theknot.com/default.htm

■ **Today's Bride**
www.todaysbride.com/

■ **Town and Country Weddings**
tncweddings.com/

■ **Ultimate Internet Wedding Guide**
www.ultimatewedding.com/

■ **WayCool Weddings Every Week**
www.waycoolweddings.com/

■ **Wedding Announcement**
www.weddingcircle.com/announce/

■ **Wedding Channel**
www.weddingchannel.com/

■ **Wedding Network**
www.weddingnetwork.com/

■ **Weddingpages**
www.the-wedding-pages.com/

■ **Weddings Online**
weddings-online.com/

■ **WedNet**
www.wednet.com/

Worldly

Take a look around the globe and don't worry if you speak only English.

■ **About Calcutta**
www.gl.umbc.edu/~achatt1/calcutta.html

■ **Africa Online**
www.africaonline.com/

■ **AfriCam**
www.africam.com/

■ **Alive! Global Network**
www.alincom.com/

■ **ArabNet**
www.arab.net/

■ **AskAsia**
www.askasia.org/

■ **Aussie Index**
www.aussie.com.au/

■ **Bali Online**
www.indo.com/

■ **Ballet Folklorico de Mexico**
www.intelnet.com.mx/ballet/

■ **Bangkok Post**
www.bangkokpost.net/

■ **Blue Window**
www.bluewin.ch/index_e.html

■ **British Columbia Archives**
www.bcarchives.gov.bc.ca/index.htm

■ **British Monarchy**
www.royal.gov.uk/

■ **Calgary Explorer**
www.calexplorer.com/

■ **Canadiana**
www.cs.cmu.edu/Unofficial/Canadiana/
README.html

■ **Caribbean Online**
www.webcom.com/earleltd/welcome.html

■ **Carrefour International**
www.carrefour.net/

■ **Chateau de Versailles**
www.chateauversailles.fr/

■ **China Pages**
www.china-pages.com/

■ **China Torch**
www.chinatorch.com/

■ **CiberCentro**
www.cibercentro.com/

■ **Czech Info Center**
www.muselik.com/czech/frame.html

■ **Devi: The Great Goddess**
www.si.edu/asia/devi/whoisdevi.htm

■ **Down Under**
www.south-pacific.com/travel-zine/

■ **Durbanet**
durbanet.aztec.co.za/

■ **Easter Island**
www.netaxs.com/~trance/rapanui.html

■ **Ellada**
www.ellada.com/

- **European Roof**
www.inch.com/~dipper/europe.html

- **Face of Russia**
www.pbs.org/weta/faceofrussia/

- **Fireball Express Suche**
www.fireball.de/

- **France Vision**
www.francevision.com/

- **Global Grocery List Project**
www.landmark-project.com/ggl.html

- **Hong Kong**
www.hongkong.org/

- **International Real Estate Directory**
www.ired.com/

- **Italia Online**
www.iol.it/

- **Japan, My Japan!**
lang.nagoya-u.ac.jp/~matsuoka/Japan.html

- **Kiwi Web**
www.chemistry.co.nz/

- **La France**
www.urec.cnrs.fr/annuaire/

- **Laurentians**
www.ietc.ca/index.htm

- **Les Chroniques de Cybérie**
www.cyberie.qc.ca/chronik/

■ **Les Pages de Paris**
www.paris.org/

■ **Living Abroad**
www.livingabroad.com/

■ **Loch Ness Monster**
www.pbs.org/wgbh/nova/lochness/

■ **Mexico**
mexico.udg.mx/

■ **Oaxaca**
www.eden.com/~tomzap

■ **Poesie Francaise**
www.webnet.fr/poesie/

■ **St. Petersburg (Russia)**
www.spb.ru/russian/

■ **Stockholm**
www.stockholm.se/

■ **Strasbourg**
www.sdv.fr/strasbourg/

■ **Tibetan Studies**
www.ciolek.com/WWWVL-
TibetanStudies.html

■ **Top of Norway**
www.ton.no/ton/

■ **United Nations**
www.un.org/

■ **Visit Your Favorite Country**
www.countries.com/

■ **World Communities**
www.einet.net/galaxy/Community/
World-Communities.html

■ **World Hello Day**
www.worldhelloday.org/

■ **World's Living Guide**
www.timeout.co.uk/

■ **Worldwide Holidays and Festivals**
www.holidayfestival.com/

■ **Your Nation**
www.your-nation.com/

■ **Yuan Ming Yuan**
www.cs.ubc.ca/spider/wang/

■ **Yupi**
www.yupi.com/

Notes:

Notes

Notes

Notes

Notes

Notes

Notes

Notes

Notes

Notes